SHETLAND SHEEPDOGS
KW-079

Overleaf: *The Shetland Sheepdog, known by numerous fanciers as the "Sheltie," has achieved a remarkable amount of popularity. Owner, Louise D. Beakes (right); Elaine Wishnow (left).*

Title page: *The Sheltie is celebrated for his charming disposition as well as his extraordinary receptiveness to his owner. Owner, Elaine Wishnow.*

Photography: *Isabelle Francais, Michael Gilroy, Robert Pearcy, Vince Serbin, and Jean D. Simmonds.*

Drawings: *Scott Boldt, Richard Crammer, Richard Davis, Andrew Prendimano, John Quinn, and Alexandra Suchenka.*

The text of this book is the result of the joint efforts of the author and editorial staff of T.F.H. Publications, Inc., which is the originator of all sections of the book except the chapters dealing with the origins of the Shetland Sheepdog, the description of the breed, and grooming. Additionally, the appearance of canine pet products in this book is for general instructive value only; the appearance of such products does not necessarily constitute an endorsement by the author, the publisher, or the owners of the dogs portrayed in this book.

t.f.h.

Distributed in the UNITED STATES by T.F.H. Publications, Inc., One T.F.H. Plaza, Neptune City, NJ 07753; in CANADA to the Pet Trade by H & L Pet Supplies Inc., 27 Kingston Crescent, Kitchener, Ontario N2B 2T6; Rolf C. Hagen Ltd., 3225 Sartelon Street, Montreal 382 Quebec; in CANADA to the Book Trade by Macmillan of Canada (A Division of Canada Publishing Corporation), 164 Commander Boulevard, Agincourt, Ontario M1S 3C7; in ENGLAND by T.F.H. Publications Limited, Cliveden House/Priors Way/Bray, Maidenhead, Berkshire SL6 2HP, England; in AUSTRALIA AND THE SOUTH PACIFIC by T.F.H. (Australia) Pty. Ltd., Box 149, Brookvale 2100 N.S.W., Australia; in NEW ZEALAND by Ross Haines & Son, Ltd., 18 Monmouth Street, Grey Lynn, Auckland 2, New Zealand; in SINGAPORE AND MALAYSIA by MPH Distributors (S) Pte., Ltd., 601 Sims Drive, #03/07/21, Singapore 1438; in the PHILIPPINES by Bio-Research, 5 Lippay Street, San Lorenzo Village, Makati Rizal; in SOUTH AFRICA by Multipet Pty. Ltd., 30 Turners Avenue, Durban 4001. Published by T.F.H. Publications, Inc. Manufactured in the United States of America by T.F.H. Publications, Inc.

SHETLAND SHEEPDOGS

BEVERLY PISANO

One of the Shetland Sheepdog's most beautiful features is his coat. The outer coat is long and straight; the mane should be abundant and particularly impressive in males. Owner, George A. Sudol.

Contents

Introducing the Shetland Sheepdog

The Shetland Sheepdog, a smaller version of the ever-popular Collie, is a dog of great appeal, be it to someone wanting a family pet, a companion, a show dog, or a hardy obedience worker. This charming breed excels in all these capacities, and is a favorite choice with households containing children.

The immensely popular standing of the Shetland Sheepdog, or Sheltie, among dog lovers is due to a number of factors, not the least of which is his endearing, bubbly personality. In addition, he is a steadfast guardian, quick to sound a warning bark at the approach of footsteps near your house. The Sheltie is wonderful around children, and can take hours of roughhousing with nary a "complaint."

This all-around breed would seem to be ideal for the person or family living in an apartment or small house, as they are much more suited to limited quarters than, say, their larger counterpart, the Collie. Still, the Sheltie will do well to be kept in a large yard all the day long, as this breed will relish the opportunity for exercise whenever it arises.

ORIGINS IN SCOTLAND

The Sheltie is descended from hearty sheepherding dogs native to the Shetland Islands off of the Scottish coast. These low-lying islands, cut by many inlets and swept by strong winds, feature a rather harsh climate, with generally cold and damp weather. In fact, so unfavorable is the climate that it is thought to be the prime factor in the bantamization of the breed, down from the larger size of the Collie-type sheepdogs, along with certain other animals, such as the Shetland Pony, and livestock, mainly sheep and cattle.

Livestock raising has long been a major industry in the Shetlands, due to the lack of arable land. Because of the rugged terrain, small breeds of shepherding dogs that can pick their way around with less danger of slipping and chance of injury have been favored.

There are historical indications that early in the 1800s a small breed of Collie was being used in the Shetlands for the care of sheep. Soon after, a number of these farm dogs or "toonies" began to appear in England, when visitors to the Shetland Islands brought them back to the mainland. It is fairly definite that these were the dogs we know today as Shetland Sheepdogs.

This breed now bears the same relationship in size and general appearance to the rough Collie as

Facing page: *For many dog owners, the Sheltie is the ideal dog—his outgoing personality complemented by his unshakable loyalty and alertness as a guard dog make him a superb pet. Owner, Louise D. Beakes.*

the Shetland Pony does to some of the larger breeds of horses. Although the resemblance between the Shetland Sheepdog and the rough Collie is marked, there are differences that can be noted.

Early on, questions arose about the best size for the breed. Many of the smaller specimens had little uniformity among themselves, and only vaguely resembled the true Collie; as such, by 1914, it was agreed that the emphasis should be placed on emulating the general appearance of the show Collie rather than on extreme smallness.

THE SHELTIE IN AMERICA

The history of Shetland Sheepdogs in America apparently "began" in 1911 when a New York breeder imported some specimens and began to advertise them. But it was not until 1929 that the present American club, the American Shetland Sheepdog Association, was organized to sponsor the breed in the United States.

Three-month-old Gallantry Amber Fair takes time out to enjoy the warmth of the autumn sun. Owner, Jean McMillan.

Bran Gay Memory Maker sits up proudly. She has distinguished herself by producing three champions. Owners, Brandol and Gayle Eads, Bran Gay Shelties.

The prime breeding problem encountered by breeders here has been concerned with their attempt to improve the "type" of the dog without increasing its size. ("Type" refers to the physicality of the dog, to the characteristics that set it apart from all other breeds. In the Doberman Pinscher, for example, the "type" of the dog would refer to its clean, chiseled structure and outline; in the Clumber Spaniel, it would refer to the short, solid, cobby body of the breed.)

Presumably, improvement of Shelties by selective breeding might have followed the normal course, but a more effective and faster method seemed to lie in crossing them with small Collies for Collie characteristics, and then breeding them down by selection.

Accordingly, some Collie crossing was done in the early years, but it was found to be very difficult to eliminate the larger specimens having good Collie type, and throwbacks to Collie size occurred all too frequently. Little if any such breeding has been undertaken recently; there is not much to be gained by such a program, for the costs are too great, with tendencies to produce oversize dogs being disastrous for a breeder and decidedly against the best interests of the breed.

Another difficulty that plagued the Sheltie fancy has been shyness. It is probable that in the past, when Shelties were chiefly used for guarding flocks, strangers were seldom seen around the farms and ranches. At any rate, some Shelties have not been friendly with strangers, and other Shelties have been shy even with their owners.

Since it is now generally recognized that shy Shelties should be avoided for breeding purposes, most of the larger kennels have generally eliminated shyness.

Description of the Sheltie

Any sheepdog to be of any use to the shepherd must be attentive, for control of sheep requires keen coordination between master and dog. The Sheltie was undoubtedly chosen and bred for the attentiveness with which he watched his master, and for his willingness to obey commands. Further, a dog who ranged widely or who followed his own desires or curiosity was of little use where the safety of a flock depended upon close teamwork. Alertness and obedience were of prime importance.

The requirements of the shepherds and the resulting selection they used in breeding have left their marks deeply imprinted upon the Sheltie. Even though Shelties seldom see a sheep today, these characteristics show plainly.

Although generalizations about the character of an animal should be avoided, it may be said that the Sheltie, as a rule, stays close to his master. Someone unfamiliar with the breed is apt to be surprised when the Sheltie, instead of launching out for himself in strange surroundings, returns promptly to his master's side. Sheltie people know that if the dog slips his leash at a show or on the street, when he can find his master again he promptly "heels," whether he has been trained to heel or not. The instinct to return quickly to the shepherd reasserts itself.

reasserts itself.

This inclination to heel is most often seen in the house, where the Sheltie unobtrusively but constantly follows his owners. He is seldom more than a few feet away, in a corner, under a chair, or behind his master, waiting for something that will require his attention.

Alertness and willingness to follow orders are necessary qualities if a dog is to keep sheep under control. The shepherd observes the tendency of the flock to move in one direction or another; he motions to his dog or whistles, and the dog must respond immediately. These traits are priceless assets in our dogs today. When a car approaches, the life of your pet may depend upon his willingness to stop or to come to you immediately. Shetland Sheepdogs are particularly easy to control; speak to them and they obey.

Anyone who watches a shepherd move a flock of sheep with the aid of his dog can hardly question the animal's intelligence. There are countless illustrations of anticipation, planning, and outguessing in the activity of the sheepdog. The Sheltie in turn shows this ability as he adjusts to our modern environment. He

Facing page: *The innocence and sincerity ever-present in the Sheltie's eyes explain the breed's growing popularity and appeal. Owner, Louise D. Beakes.*

quickly learns to adapt to things and people, while he fits himself into situations with a minimum of fuss.

There is another trait the Sheltie seems to have acquired from his life with the Shetland people and their flocks of past centuries. He is not a fighter, for the dog who challenged every newcomer or threatened to fight at every lift of a tail would abandon the flock to outdo each opponent. It is hard to say just what arouses the antagonism of a dog, but it is a curious thing that Shelties will very seldom either start or become involved in a fight. This is a welcome virtue for those of us who do not like to spend our lives preventing dog fights.

But this does not mean the Sheltie will not use his abilities to defend his master or his family if the need arises: there are many cases in which Shelties have risen to emergencies and performed heroically in the face of danger. Shelties have killed snakes, notified parents of dangers to their children, kept their young charges out of the paths of trouble, and, in the course of their daily business, have undoubtedly discouraged many an intended trespasser.

Small though he is, the Sheltie is constitutionally strong. His ancestors were working dogs of rugged strength, and the conditions under which they lived eliminated many dogs that would have survived only in more temperate climates and more pampered circumstances.

The Sheltie needs no extra attention; he thrives under almost any conditions. The ideal home for a Sheltie is with a family in a small house in the suburbs. There should be a third to half an acre of ground that has a fenced run so that he can exercise alone in safety. Although he is ideal as a children's pet, and small enough

Ch. Marwal Struttin' The Blues, by Am. and Can. Ch. Macdega Mainstay ex Marwal Bluesette. Bred by Marwal Kennels, Margaret and Walt Huening.

Can. Ch. Genson's Intrepid Man (on the left) and Can. Ch. Gray Dawn Reveille (on the right) relax on a rocky bank overlooking the sea to enjoy the sunset. Both dogs are well-known Best in Show winners in Canada.

for even the youngest to handle him on a leash or play with boisterously, most children have to be watched at first to be sure they are gentle with him. His exercise run, too, should not be where children passing by can tease him.

HOUSING AND EXERCISING THE SHELTIE

A Shetland Sheepdog can get sufficient exercise in the house. When the housewife is busy at her tasks, the Sheltie is busy too: he superintends the arrival of the milk, the mail, and the comings and goings of the other members of the family. A puppy should spend more time out of doors, going out for a few minutes frequently, but a grown Sheltie can get all the fresh air he needs in a couple of fifteen- or twenty-minute free runs in the yard daily.

Grown Shelties can endure the cold through most northern winters if they have snug quarters free from drafts. Make sure that the dog house is not too large for him, that it has wind-tight and cold resistant walls, clean bedding, and a draped or baffled opening away from the prevailing winds. However, dogs, no more than people, shouldn't be expected to spend the day in a warm house and then shiver in an unheated, drafty shack all night. If you love your Sheltie, train him to be a house dog; don't send him out to spend the night in the backyard, while you sleep comfortably warm in the house!

All he really needs is a box in a warm corner of the house. His bed should be away from drafts, but not in front of the radiator. If you take the trouble to train him properly he will sleep wherever you wish—in his box or on your bed!

A portrait of Can. Ch. Hi-Hope MacDee's Marsea, Can. and Am. C.D. Mary MacDonald, owner.

Shelties are naturally intelligent, easily taught and generally obedient. For that reason many Shelties are to be found in dog training classes and obedience classes at dog shows. But the Sheltie owner does not have to take his dog to the obedience classes to learn to control him. Firmness and a positive "No!" expressed just as your Sheltie is about to indulge himself in some mischief will break bad habits and teach your Sheltie to behave himself.

Teaching tricks (for example, "speaking," jumping, catching balls, fetching, rolling over) is merely the development of natural traits. With a pat on the head when he catches the ball, a tidbit or good petting when he rolls over (with your help at first, perhaps), eventually he can be persuaded to catch anything you throw to him, and he will roll over when you tell him to. These are things that dogs do themselves; we have only taught them to do them when we ask.

Obedience, or the act of doing things in response to a command rather than when the dog chooses to do them, is in fact the first step in training for more complicated

Ch. Chicwin's Classic Conqueror, by Ch. Sovereign Ring's Legacy ex Ch. Chicwin's Promised Conquest. Breeder-owner, Fred Gordon, Chicwin Shetland Sheepdogs.

jobs, such as herding stock. The shepherd trains his Sheltie to "Come," "Stay," and "Go," in the direction to which he is waved, before he is allowed near the animals he is being trained for. Later, with the stock the shepherd gives his instructions with these commands, and the Sheltie obediently follows them. A dog who cannot be controlled is of no use with livestock.

CURING THE SHELTIE'S BAD HABITS

Habitual barking may usually be stopped if you take the trouble to insist on it. If your Sheltie becomes so interested in barking that you cannot get his attention, it may be necessary to clap your hands, shout at him, or threaten him with a folded newspaper.

Although a dog's owner or family may stop him from barking when it is just a "running off at the mouth," if your Sheltie believes his barking is justified, he may refuse to stop. Thus, a Sheltie who is barking at the menace of a stranger would not be likely to stop because of anything the stranger did, or threatened to do, and he might not stop for you, if he thought you were in any danger.

Nervousness is sometimes manifested by barking, in which case a dog can seldom control himself. He may stop for a few minutes, only to start right up again. It may be necessary to remove him from the room so he cannot see or hear what he was initially barking at.

USING THE SHELTIE STANDARD

For every breed of dog accepted by the American Kennel Club, which is the main dog-registering body in the United States, there is a written standard. Likewise, other national kennel clubs have developed standards for all the breeds recognized by each of those organizations. These standards describe the "ideal" specimen of each breed, exemplifying those dogs that are strived for by conscientious breeders.

It is recommended that the owner or prospective owner of a Shetland Sheepdog become familiar with the official standard of the national club under which the dog is registered. If you choose to have a show prospect Shetland Sheepdog, there are specifics within the standard that you should study carefully for help in selecting the right dog for you. (If you are buying a puppy, use the standard as a means of evaluating the sire and dam of that puppy . Even if you do not plan to show your Sheltie, you are likely to be interested in comparing your dog to the description of the perfect Shetland Sheepdog.

The requirements as set forth in the official standards of the American Kennel Club and the Kennel Club of Great Britain are essentially the same. For that reason, as well as for the sake of brevity, only a version of the AKC standard is included in this book. If your Shetland Sheepdog is registered in England or is to be shown on an international basis, it would be advantageous for you to acquire a copy of the appropriate standard.

Following is an example of a standard for the Shetland Sheepdog. It is important to be aware that standards are different from country to country and from registry to registry and that they change from time to time, in phrasing and subsequent content. If you are serious about showing your Sheltie, your local club will be able to provide you with a copy of the most up-to-date standard and any other relevant information.

Facing page: *Whether your Sheltie is a show dog, a herd dog, or just a family pet, perusing the standard can be both interesting and informative. Owner, Elaine Wishnow.*

AKC STANDARD FOR THE SHETLAND SHEEPDOG

General Description: The Shetland Sheepdog is a small, alert, rough-coated, longhaired working dog. He must be sound, agile and sturdy. The outline should be so symmetrical that no part appears out of proportion to the whole. Dogs should appear masculine; bitches, feminine.

Size: The Shetland Sheepdog should stand between 13 and 16 inches at the shoulder. Note: Height is determined by a line perpendicular to the ground from the top of the shoulder blades, the dog standing naturally, with forelegs parallel to line of measurement. ***Disqualification:*** *Heights below or above the desired size range are to be disqualified from the show ring.*

Coat: The coat should be double, the outer coat consisting of long, straight, harsh hair; the undercoat short, furry, and so dense as to give the entire coat its "stand-off" quality. The hair on face, tips of ears and feet should be smooth. Mane and frill should be abundant, and particularly impressive in males. The forelegs, well feathered, the hind legs, heavily so, but smooth below the hock joint. Hair on tail, profuse. Note: Excess hair on ears, feet, and on hocks may be trimmed for the show ring. ***Faults:*** *Coat short or flat, in whole or in part; wavy, curly, soft or silky. Lack of undercoat. Smooth-coated specimens.*

Color: Black, blue merle, and sable (ranging from golden through mahogany); marked with varying amount of white and/or tan. ***Faults:*** *Rustiness in a black or blue coat. Washed out or degenerate colors, such as pale sable and faded blue. Self-color in the case of blue merle, that is, without any merling or mottling and generally appearing as a faded or dilute tri-color. Conspicuous white body spots. Specimens with more than 50 percent white shall be so severely penalized as to effectively eliminate them from competition.* ***Disqualification:*** *Brindle.*

Temperament: The Shetland Sheepdog is intensely loyal, affectionate, and responsive to his owner. However, he may be reserved toward strangers but not to the point of showing fear or cringing in the ring. ***Faults:*** *Shyness, timidity, or nervousness. Stubbornness, snappiness, or ill temper.*

Head: The head should be refined and its shape, when viewed from top or side, be a long, blunt wedge tapering slightly from ears to nose, which must be black. Skull and Muzzle: Top of skull should be flat, showing no prominence at nuchal crest (the top of the occiput). Cheeks should be flat and should merge smoothly into a well-rounded muzzle. Skull and muzzle should be of equal length, balance point being inner

The Sheltie has excelled in obedience trials as it has on the field. This is Ch. Mainstay Rumor Has It, co-owned by Jo Ann McNeal and Stephen W. Barger.

corner of eye. In profile the top line of skull should parallel the top line of muzzle, but on a higher plane due to the presence of a slight but definite stop. Jaws clean and powerful. The deep, well-developed under-jaw, rounded at chin, should extend to base of nostril. Lips tight. Upper and lower lips must meet and fit smoothly together all the way around. Teeth level and evenly spaced. Scissors bite. ***Faults:*** *Two-angled head. Too prominent stop, or no stop. Overfill below, between, or above eyes. Prominent nuchal crest. Domed skull. Prominent cheekbones. Snipy muzzle. Short, receding, or shallow under-jaw, lacking breadth and depth. Overshot or undershot, missing or crooked teeth. Teeth visible when mouth is closed.*

Eyes: Medium size with dark, almond-shaped rims, set somewhat obliquely in skull. Color must be dark, with blue or merle eyes permissible in blue merles only. ***Faults:*** *Light, round, large or too small. Prominent haws.*

Ears: Small and flexible, placed high, carried three-fourths erect, with tips breaking forward. When in repose the ears fold lengthwise and are thrown back into the frill. ***Faults:*** *Set too low. Hound, prick, bat, twisted ears. Leather too thick or too thin.*

Expression: Contours and chiseling of the head, the shape, set and use of ears, the placement, shape and color of the eyes, combine to produce expression. Normally the expression should be alert, gentle, intelligent and questioning. Toward strangers the eyes should show watchfulness and reserve, but no fear.

The three-quarter carriage of the Sheltie's ears has become characteristic of the breed. This is Ch. Markris Red Baron of Edlen, owned by Edmund and Helen Scherer.

Neck: Neck should be muscular, arched, and of sufficient length to carry the head proudly. ***Faults:*** *Too short and thick.*

Body: In overall appearance the body should appear moderately long as measured from shoulder joint to ischium (rearmost extremity of the pelvic bone), but much of this length is actually due to the proper angulation and breadth of the shoulder and hindquarter, as the back itself should be comparatively short. Back should be level and strongly muscled. Chest should be deep, the brisket reaching to point of elbow. The ribs should be well sprung, but flattened at their lower half to allow free play of the foreleg and shoulder. Abdomen moderately tucked up. ***Faults:*** *Back too long, too short, swayed or roached. Barrel ribs. Slabside. Chest narrow and/or too shallow.*

Forequarters: From the withers the shoulder blades should slope at a 45-degree angle forward and downward to the shoulder joints. At the withers they are separated only by the vertebra, but they must slope outward sufficiently to accommodate the desired spring of rib. The upper arm should join the shoulder blade at as nearly as

This exceptional Sheltie is Ch. Shadowdale Come Fly With Me at six months of age, owned by Evelyn K. Basnicki.

possible a right angle. Elbow joint should be equidistant from the ground or from the withers. Forelegs straight viewed from all angles, muscular and clean, and of strong bone. Pasterns very strong, sinewy and flexible. Dewclaws may be removed. ***Faults:*** *Insufficient angulation between shoulder and upper arm. Upper arm too short. Lack of outward slope of shoulders. Loose shoulders. Turning in or out of elbows. Crooked legs. Light bone.*

Feet (Front and Hind): Feet should be oval and compact with the toes well arched and fitting tightly together. Pads deep and tough, nails hard and strong.

Faults: *Feet turning in or out. Splay-feet. Hare-feet. Cat-feet.*

Hindquarters: There should be a slight arch at the loins, and the croup should slope gradually to the rear. The hipbone (pelvis) should be set at a 30-degree angle to the spine. The thigh should be broad and muscular.

The thighbone should be set into the pelvis at a right angle corresponding to the angle of the shoulder blade and upper arm. Stifle bones join the thighbone and should be distinctly angled at the stifle joint. The overall length of the stifle should at least equal the length of the thighbone, and preferably should slightly exceed it. Hock joint should be clean-cut, angular, sinewy, with good bone and strong ligamentation. The hock (metatarsus) should be short and straight viewed from all angles. Dewclaws should be removed. ***Faults:*** *Croup higher than withers. Croup too straight or too steep. Narrow thighs. Cowhocks. Hocks turning out. Poorly defined hock joint.*

Tail: The tail should be sufficiently long so that when it is laid along the back edge of the hind legs the last vertebra will reach the hock joint. Carriage of tail at rest is straight down or in a slight upward curve. When the dog is alert the tail is normally lifted, but it should not be curved forward over the back. ***Faults:*** *Too short. Twisted at end.*

Gait: The trotting gait of the Shetland Sheepdog should denote effortless speed and smoothness. There should be no jerkiness, nor stiff, stilted, up-and-down movement. The drive should be from the rear, true and straight, dependent upon correct angulation, musculation, and ligamentation of the entire hindquarter, thus allowing the dog to reach well under his body with his hind foot and propel himself forward. Reach of stride of the foreleg is dependent upon correct angulation, musculation and ligamentation of the forequarters, together with correct width of chest and construction of rib cage. The foot should be lifted only enough to clear the ground as the leg swings forward. Viewed from the front, both forelegs and hind legs should move forward almost perpendicular to ground at the walk, slanting a little inward at a slow trot, until at a swift trot the feet are brought so far inward toward center line of body that the tracks left show two parallel lines of footprints actually touching a center line at their inner edges. There should be no crossing of the feet nor throwing of the weight from side to side. ***Faults:*** *Stiff, short steps, with a choppy, jerky movement. Mincing steps, with a hopping up and down, or a balancing of weight from side to side (often erroneously admired as a "dancing gait" but permissible in young puppies). Lifting of front feet in hackneylike action, resulting in loss of speed and energy. Pacing gait.*

Facing page: *Shelties are very affectionate and responsive companions. Ch. Chicwin's Chelsea exhibits flawless head type as well as an irresistibly warm expression. Owner-bred by Fred Gordon, Chicwin Shetland Sheepdogs.*

NOTES ABOUT THE BRITISH STANDARD

The Kennel Club standard, while similar to the AKC standard in most respects, specifically calls for ideal heights to be 14½ for dogs and 14 inches for bitches, with anything more than an inch above those measurements to be considered as a serious fault. The Kennel Club also further describes the Shetland Sheepdog's ears as being moderately wide at the base and set fairly close together on the top of the skull.

Of particular interest to the owner of a British-registered dog is a section of the Kennel Club standard that deals with characteristics and general appearance. That section reads as follows:

"To enable the Shetland Sheepdog to fulfill its natural bent for sheepdog work, its physical structure should be on the lines of strength and activity, free from cloddiness and without any trace of coarseness. Although the desired type is similar to that of the Rough Collie there are marked differences that must be noted. . .

"The Shetland Sheepdog should show affection and response to his owner, he may show reserve to strangers but not to the point of nervousness.

"The Shetland Sheepdog should instantly appeal as a dog of great beauty, intelligence and alertness. Action, lithe and graceful with speed and jumping power great for its size. The outline should be symmetrical so that no part appears out of proportion to the whole. An abundance of coat, mane and frill, with shapeliness of head and sweetness of expression all combine to present the ideal Shetland Sheepdog that will inspire and secure admiration."

In temperament, the Shetland Sheepdog is neither shy and timid nor snappy and stubborn. This is Ch. Rickgarbob Dianamation, owner-bred by Bob Carlough and Mrs. Marie Carlough.

To illustrate the size difference between the two breeds, here stands a Collie (right) next to a Shetland Sheepdog (left). For the person who has always loved the Collie but does not have the requisite amount of space to keep one, the Sheltie is unmistakably the dog for you.

Grooming the Sheltie

A Sheltie can go from puppyhood to old age, if necessary, with almost no "grooming" as dog fanciers think of it. From year to year nature's processes slough off the old coats and replace them with new.

I have seen Shelties that looked as if their owners relied on nature to take care of them. They had a good percentage of last winter's coat, and perhaps some from the year before that, hanging in snarls and mats. But most of us like the handsome appearance of our Sheltie; although little work is required to keep his coat in good condition, it is ridiculous to neglect it.

The principal grooming that a Sheltie needs is having his coat brushed and the dead coat removed occasionally. Every dog—be he long- or short-coated—regularly sheds his old hair and replaces it with new. The growth of a coat depends on many things, but in general the old coat is shed in late spring, to be replaced in time for winter.

The start of shedding will be noticed when a few hairs come out on rugs or clothing; at this time brushing, perhaps once a week, with a stiff brush will be sufficient. At all other times, a natural bristle brush is the best one to use, as it is kind to the hair, eliminating breakage, and it allows for the coat's natural oils to be distributed evenly.

Regular brushing helps the Sheltie's appearance greatly. The gentle pulling and stroking of the brush also serves to stimulate the flow of natural oil along the hair and spreads it uniformly over the coat. A well-brushed coat not only looks brushed, but it also has a degree of brilliance partly, at least, in proportion to the diligence and the industry of the brusher.

For the more fastidious, further grooming involves a bit of barbering. Shelties who are to be shown generally have their whiskers trimmed off close to the fur, including the long ones above the eyes and those on the Adam's apple. These long, black hairs sticking out do not add anything to the dog's appearance, however useful they may have once been in keeping him out of trouble. (They are supposed to be a device for keeping his nose out of mischief, but they are not very effective).

Hair is also trimmed from between the pads of the feet, from the fetlocks, and up the hind legs to the hocks. Feathers along the back of the front legs and the panties should not be trimmed, though a long hair or two might be removed to even them up.

What is done to the ears will depend upon whether they are

Facing page: *In order to keep your Sheltie looking his best, regular grooming habits must be adhered to. Owner, Louise D. Beakes.*

low, erect, or correctly tipped over. Ear carriage is very important in a Sheltie. "Natural" ears are carried semi-erect (just the tips folding forward for attention), but few Shelties are that way without assistance. The degree of erectness depends upon the strength of a small muscle in the ear, and the weight of the ear itself. Shelties vary in their ear carriage, from those with ears that hang down like a hound's to those that stick up straight like a mule's. If they tend to hang too low, they may be encouraged to rise by trimming or stripping off the weight of the hair, and if they tend to stand straight up they may be trained to bend over by weighting them. Ask a breeder who shows dogs, your veterinarian, or a professional groomer about this "weighting" procedure.

Grooming may go to greater lengths, such as scraping the teeth to remove tartar and filing or clipping toenails, but these things are better left to professionals. They will, of course, do the whole job for you, should you so desire, but never let them clip a Sheltie "for the summer."

We know now that external parasites are potential carriers of disease. Look your dog over critically. If he simply needs a flea powder, apply it. But if he looks as if he might have something worse—by all means take him to your veterinarian before it gets out of hand. Mange, mites, lice, ticks, and similar parasites should not be fooled with.

Bathing is seldom necessary or desirable with a Sheltie, as there isn't much that gets through his

A double coat consisting of long, straight, harsh hair on the outer and short, furry, dense hair on the inner is desirable according to the standard. Sterling's Enchanted Spirit is owned by Debra Elkin, Enchanted Shelties.

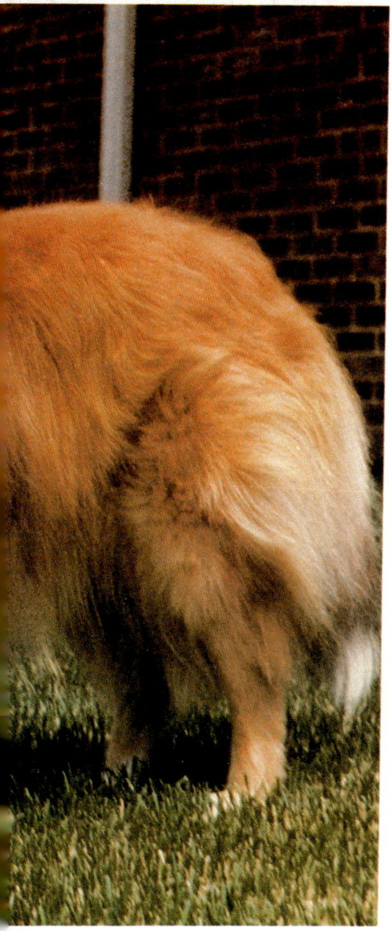

undercoat. Dogs do not perspire as we do, and though constant replacement of body cells does yield some scurf, it is nothing like dandruff.

Except when the Sheltie has somehow gotten plastered with mud, or when you want to show him (and not always then, for a bath tends to loosen the coat, which would be disastrous for a show) no bathing should be undertaken.

But, if you must bathe him, the proper way is in a tub with about two or three inches of warm (never hot) water, dipping or sponging it over him. A good lather of a mild dog soap is worked up and rinsed off thoroughly with warm water. Because a dog's skin is different from a human being's in a number of ways, it is always best to use soaps and shampoos formulated specifically for canine use; do not use human-type cleansing products. Rinsing is easiest with a hose, but it may be done with a dipper, replenishing the tub with clean water as needed. Washing and rinsing the dog's head, and around his eyes, should be left for last, as it must be done with great care, so as not to get soap or water into the dog's eyes or ears. To eliminate this potentially irritating problem, apply a few drops of mineral oil into each of the dog's eyes, and a cotton ball in each ear. Be sure not to go too deeply into the ear with the cotton.

After the final rinse, which should assure that no trace of soapy residue remains as a source of irritation, rub the Sheltie dry with a thick terry towel, using brisk strokes. The completion of the drying can be achieved by the use of a blow dryer, held a distance of at least 12 inches from the coat. Or, in warm, sunny weather, you may let the Sheltie out of doors to dry in the yard.

A well-groomed Sheltie is a source of true joy and pride to his owner. This handsome pair belongs to Patricia B. Marchello.

Selecting Your Dog

Now that you have decided which dog breed suits your needs, your lifestyle, and your own temperament, there will be much to consider before you make your final purchase. Buying a puppy on impulse may only cause heartbreak later on; it makes better sense to put some real thought into your canine investment, especially since it is likely that he will share many happy years with you. Which individual will you choose as your adoring companion? Ask yourself some questions as you analyze your needs and preferences for a dog, read all that you can about your particular breed, and visit as many dog shows as possible. At the shows you will be surrounded by people who can give you all the details about the breed you are interested in buying. Decide if you want a household pet, a dog for breeding, or a show dog. Would you prefer a male or female? Puppy or adult?

If you buy from a breeder, ask him to help you with your decision. When you have settled on the dog you want, discuss with him the dog's temperament, the animal's positive and negative aspects, any health problems it might have, its feeding and grooming requirements, and whether the dog has been immunized. Reputable breeders will be willing to answer any questions you might have that pertain to the dog you have selected, and often they will make themselves available if you call for advice or if you encounter problems after you've made your purchase.

Good natured and frolicsome describe well Sweet Harmony of Elden as a puppy. Owners, Edmund and Helen Scherer, Elden Shelties.

Some dog lovers are attracted to several breeds, and mixed breeds and other animals as well! If all are raised together from infancy, there should be harmony in your household.

Most breeders want to see their dogs placed in loving, responsible homes; they are careful about who buys their animals. So as the dog's new owner, prepare yourself for some interrogation from the breeder.

WHERE TO BUY

You can choose among several places to buy your dog. Many people think of their local pet shop as the first source for buying a puppy, and very often they're right; you should remember, however, that a pet shop cannot possibly stock all breeds of dog. If your pet shop does not carry the type of dog you desire, there are other places to look. One is a kennel whose business is breeding show-quality dogs; such kennels may have extra pups for sale. Another source is the one-dog owner who wants to sell the puppies from an occasional litter to pay the expenses of his small-scale breeding operation. To find such kennels and part-time breeders and hobbyists, check the classified section of your local newspaper or look in your telephone directory.

Whichever source you choose, you can usually tell in a very short time whether the puppies will make healthy and happy pets. If they are clean, plump, and lively, they are probably in good health. At the breeder's you will have the advantage of seeing the puppies' dam and perhaps their sire and other relatives. Remember that the mother, having just raised a demanding family, may not be looking her best; but if she is sturdy, friendly, and well-mannered, her puppies should be too. If you feel that something is lacking in the care or condition of the dogs, it is better to look elsewhere than to buy hastily and regret it afterward. Buy a healthy dog with a good disposition, one that has been

This Belle Mount Sheltie puppy is all ready to jet to his new home. One should be fully prepared for the arrival of a new dog so that his first night in your home will be a pleasant and less trying one. Owner, Alice A. Burhans.

This frisky box of Sheltie pups is bound to delight any dog owner—their playful mischief is always great fun to watch!

properly socialized and likes being around people.

If you cannot find the dog you want locally, write to the secretary of the national breed club or kennel club and ask for names of breeders near you or to whom you can write for information. Puppies are often shipped, sight unseen, from reputable breeders. In these instances, pictures and pedigree information are usually sent beforehand to help you decide. Breeders can supply you with further details and helpful guidance, if you require it. Many breed clubs provide a puppy referral service, so you may want to look into this before making your final decision.

PET OR SHOW DOG

Conscientious breeders strive to maintain those desirable qualities in their breed. At the same time, they are always working to improve on what they have already achieved, and they do this by referring to the breed standard of perfection. The standard describes the ideal dog, and those animals that come close to the ideal are generally selected as show

How often have you gone into a pet shop in search of that special dog breed? It is difficult to make a decision, particularly when every pooch cries, "buy me!"

stock; those that do not are culled and sold as pets. Keep in mind that pet-quality purebred dogs are in no way less healthy or attractive than show-quality specimens. It's just that the pet may have undesirable features (such as ears that are too large or eyes that are the wrong color for its breed) which would be faults in the show ring. Often these so-called "flaws" are detectable only by experienced breeders or show judges. Naturally the more perfect animal, in terms of its breed standard, will cost more—even though he seems almost identical to his pet-quality littermate.

If you think you may eventually want to show your dog or raise a litter of puppies, by all means buy the best you can afford. You will save expense and disappointment later on. However, if the puppy is strictly to be a pet for the children, or a companion for you, you can afford to look for a bargain. The pup which is not show material, or the older pup for which there is often less demand, or the grown dog which is not being used for breeding are occasionally available and offer opportunities to save money. Remember that your initial investment may be a bargain, but it takes good food and care—and plenty of both—to raise a healthy, vigorous puppy through its adulthood.

Starhaven's Collector's Item at two months of age enjoys the frivolous days of puppyhood. Owners, Carl and Amy Langhorst, Starhaven Kennels.

Facing page: *The gentle and good-mannered personality of the Shetland Sheepdog makes him a wonderful pet for children—they are affectionate companions as well as reliable guardians.*

The price you pay for your dog is little compared to the love and devotion he will return over the many years he'll be with you. With proper care and affection your pup should live to a ripe old age; thanks to modern veterinary science and improvements in canine nutrition, today dogs are better maintained and live longer. It is not uncommon to see dogs living well into their teens.

If you are planning to travel with your dog—to dog shows, to the vet, or on vacation—by all means place him in a safe carrier.

MALE OR FEMALE

If you intend to breed your dog someday, by all means buy a female. You can find a suitable mate without difficulty when the time comes, and you'll have the pleasure of raising a litter of puppies. If you don't want to raise puppies, however, your female should be spayed so that she will remain a healthy, lively pet. Similarly, a male purchased as a pet, rather than as a stud dog, should be castrated. The female is smaller than the male and generally quieter. She has less tendency to roam in search of romance, but a properly

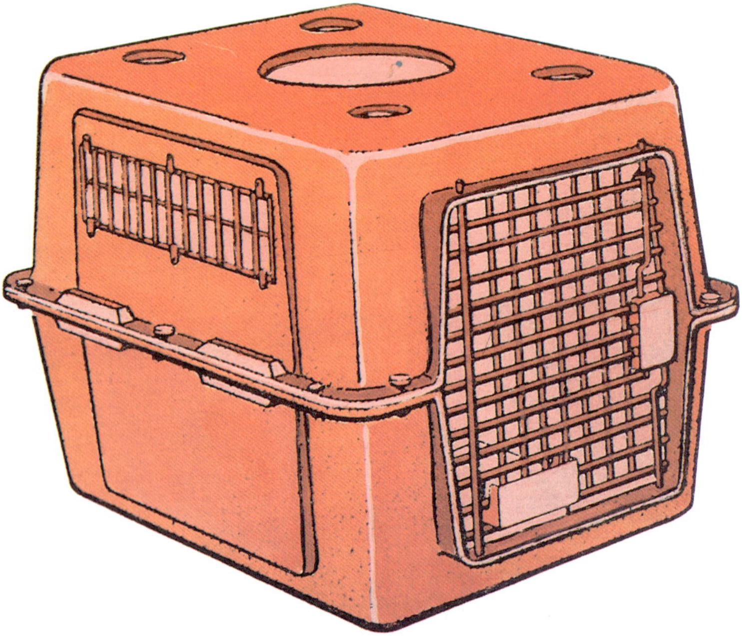

If you believe in zodiac signs, then make sure you select a dog that has been born in a month that is compatible with your own birthday!

trained male can be a charming pet and has a certain difference in temperament that is appealing to many people. Male versus female is chiefly a matter of personal choice; both make fine companions.

ADULT OR PUP

Whether to buy a grown dog or a young puppy is another question. It is undeniably fun to watch your dog grow from a lively pup to a mature, dignified dog. If you don't have the time to spend on the more frequent meals, housebreaking, and other training a puppy needs in order to become a dog you can be proud of, then choose an older, partly-trained adolescent or a grown dog. If you want a show dog, remember that no one, not even an expert, can predict with one hundred percent accuracy what a puppy will be like when he grows up. The dog may seem to exhibit show potential *most* of the time, but six months is the earliest age for the would-be exhibitor to select a prospect and know that its future is in the show ring.

If you have a small child, it is best to get a puppy big enough to defend itself, one not less than four or five months old. Older children will enjoy playing with and helping to take care of a baby pup; but at less than four months, a puppy wants to do little else but eat and sleep, and he must be protected from teasing and overtiring. You cannot expect a very young child to understand that a puppy is a fragile living being; to the youngster he is a toy like his

This priceless, sparkling litter belongs to dam Velveteen Gold Dust, owned by Evelyn Byers. The puppy you chose should be alert and of pleasant disposition.

The kind and easygoing temperament of the Sheltie makes him likeable to just about everyone!

stuffed dog. Children, therefore, must learn how to handle and care for their young pets.

We recommend you start with a puppy so that you can raise and train it according to the rules you have established in your own home. While a dog is young, its behavior can be more easily shaped by the owner, whereas an older dog , although trainable, may be a bit set in his ways.

WHAT TO LOOK FOR IN A PUPPY

In choosing a puppy, assuming that it comes from healthy, well-bred parents, look for one that is friendly and outgoing. The biggest pup in the litter is apt to be somewhat coarse as a grown dog, while the appealing "runt of the litter" may turn out to be a timid shadow—or have a Napoleonic complex! If you want a show dog and have no experience in choosing a prospect, study the breed standard and listen carefully to the breeder on the finer points of show conformation. A breeder's prices will be in accord with his puppies' expected worth, and he will be honest with you about each pup's potential because it is to his own advantage. He wants his top-quality show puppies placed in the public eye to reflect glory on him—and to attract future buyers. Why should he sell a potential show champion to someone who just wants a pet?

Now that you have paid your money and made your choice, you are ready to depart with puppy, papers, and instructions. Make sure that you know the youngster's feeding routine, and take along some of his food. For the trip home, place him in a comfortable, sturdy carrier. Do not drive home with a puppy on your lap! If you'll be travelling for a few hours, at the very least bring along a bottle of water from the breeder and a small water dish.

PEDIGREE AND REGISTRATION

Owners of puppies are often misled by sellers with such ruses as leading the owner to believe his dog is something special. The term *pedigree papers* is quite different from the term *registration papers.* A pedigree is nothing more than a statement made by the breeder of the dog; and it is written on special pedigree blanks, which are readily available from any pet shop or breed club, with the names of several generations from which the new puppy comes. It records your puppy's ancestry and other important data, such as the pup's date of birth, its breed, its sex, its sire and dam, the name and address of its breeder, and so on. If your dog has had purebred champions in his background, then the pedigree papers are valuable as evidence of the good breeding behind your dog; but if the names on the pedigree paper are meaningless, then so is the paper itself. Just because a dog has a pedigree doesn't necessarily mean he is registered with a kennel club.

Registration papers from the American Kennel Club in the United States or the Kennel Club in Great Britain attest to the fact that the mother and father of your puppy were purebred dogs of the breed represented by your puppy and that they were registered with a particular club. Normally every registered dog also has a complete pedigree available. Registration papers,

Facing page: *The scene is the Westminster Kennel Club dog show, which is held every year at Madison Square Garden in New York. It is the premier dog show in the United States; in Great Britain, the equivalent show is Crufts. Photo, Isabelle Francais.*

RING 1
RING 7
WKC
WKC
WKC
WKC

which you receive when you buy a puppy, merely enable you to register your puppy. Usually the breeder has registered only the litter, so it is the new owner's responsibility to register and name an individual pup. The papers should be filled out and sent to the appropriate address printed on the application, along with the fee required for the registration. A certificate of registration will then be sent to you.

Pedigree and registration, by the way, have nothing to do with licensing, which is a local regulation applying to purebred and mongrel alike. Find out what the local ordinance is in your town or city and how it applies to your dog; then buy a license and keep it on your dog's collar for identification.

For Ch. Severn Comedy Tonight, winning is no laughing matter! Owner, Joanne G. Timpany.

The New Family Member

A puppy as handsome and delightful as future champion SumerSong Winter Shadows would be a fine addition to any home. Owner-bred by Peggy and Jan Haderlie, SumerSong Shelties.

At long last, the day you have all been waiting for, your new puppy will make its grand entrance into your home. Before you bring your companion to its new residence, however, you must plan carefully for its arrival. Keep in mind that the puppy will need

Still popular is the wooden dog house, a place in which your dog can retreat from the world. If you buy or build one, make sure it is sturdy and that it offers sufficient protection from the elements.

time to adjust to life with a different owner. He may seem a bit apprehensive about the strange surroundings in which he finds himself, having spent the first few weeks of life with his dam and littermates, but in a couple of days, with love and patience on your part, the transition will be complete.

First impressions are important, especially from the puppy's point of view, and these may very well set the pattern of his future relationship with you. You must be consistent, always, in the way you handle your pet so that he learns what is expected of him. He must come to trust and respect you as his keeper and master. Provide him with proper care and attention, and you will be rewarded with a loyal companion for many years. Considering the needs of your puppy and planning ahead will surely make the change from his former home to his new one easier.

ADVANCE PREPARATION

In preparing for your puppy's arrival, perhaps more important than anything else is to find out from the seller how the pup was maintained. What brand of food was offered and when and how often was the puppy fed? Has the pup been housebroken; if so, what method was employed?

Attempt to continue whatever routine was started by the person from whom you bought your puppy, then, gradually, you can make those changes that suit you and your lifestyle. If, for example, the puppy has been paper trained, plan to stock up on newspaper. Place this newspaper toilet facility in a selected spot so that your puppy learns to use the designated area as its "bathroom." And keep on hand a supply of the dog food to which he is accustomed, as a sudden switch to new food could cause digestive upsets.

Every dog should have his own bed. Pet shops stock beds of all sizes and shapes, so there is sure to be one suitable for your canine pal.

Another consideration is sleeping and resting quarters. Be sure to supply a dog bed for your pup, and introduce him to his special cozy corner so that he knows where to retire when he feels like taking a snooze. You'll need to buy a collar (or harness) and leash, a safe chew item (such as Nylabone® or Gumabone®), and a few grooming tools as well. A couple of sturdy feeding dishes, one for food and one for water, will be needed; and it will be necessary, beforehand, to set up a feeding station.

FINDING A VETERINARIAN

An important part of your preparations should include finding a local veterinarian who can provide quality health care in the form of routine check-ups,

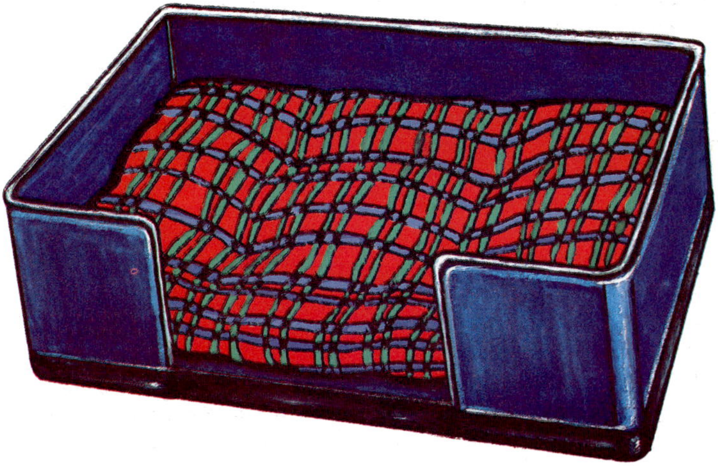

inoculations, and prompt medical attention in case of illness or an emergency. Find out if the animal you have selected has been vaccinated against canine diseases, and make certain you secure all health certificates at the time of purchase. This information will be valuable to your veterinarian, who will want to know the puppy's complete medical history. Incidentally, don't wait until your puppy becomes sick before you seek the services of a vet; make an appointment for your pup before or soon after he takes up residence with you so that he starts out with a clean bill of health in his new home.

CHILDREN AND PUPPIES

Prepare the young members of the household on pet care. Children should learn not only to love their charges but to respect them and treat them with the consideration one would give all living things. It must be emphasized to youngsters that the puppy has certain needs, just as humans have, and all family members must take an active role in ensuring that these needs are met. Someone must feed the puppy. Someone must walk him a couple of times a day or clean up after him if he is trained to relieve himself on newspaper. Someone must groom his coat, clean his ears, and clip his nails from time to time. Someone must see to it that the puppy gets sufficient exercise and attention each day.

A child who has a pet to care for learns responsibility; nonetheless, parental guidance is an essential part of his learning experience. Many a child has been known to "love a pet to death," squeezing and hugging the animal in ways which are irritating or even painful. Others have been found guilty of teasing, perhaps unintentionally, and disturbing their pet while the animal is eating or resting. One must teach a child, therefore, when and how to gently stroke and fondle a puppy. In time, the child can learn how to carefully pick up and handle the pup. A dog should always be supported with both hands, *not* lifted by the scruff of the neck. One hand placed under the chest, between the front legs, and the other hand supporting the dog's rear end will be comfortable and will restrain the animal as you hold and carry him. Always demonstrate to children the proper way to lift a dog.

BE A GOOD NEIGHBOR

For the sake of your dog's safety and well being, don't allow him to wander onto the property of others. Keep him confined at all times to your own yard or indoors where he won't become a nuisance. Consider what

In his original capacity as a sheep herder, the Sheltie was required to be obedient and attentive. Today's Shelties have retained both these positive traits. Owner, Patricia B. Marchello.

dangers lie ahead for an unleashed dog that has total freedom of the great outdoors, particularly when he is unsupervised by his master. There are cars and trucks to dodge on the streets and highways. There are stray animals with which to wrangle. There are poisons all around, such as car antifreeze in driveways or toxic plants and shrubs, which, if swallowed, could prove fatal. There are dognappers and sadistic people who may steal or bring harm to your beloved pet. In short, there are all sorts of nasty things waiting to hurt him. Did you know that if your dog consumes rotting garbage, there is the possibility he could go into shock or even die? And are you aware that a dog left to roam in a wooded area or field could become infected with any number of parasites if he plays with or ingests some small prey, such as a rabbit, that might be carrying these parasitic organisms? A thorn from a rosebush imbedded in the dog's foot pad, tar from a newly paved road stuck to his coat, or a wound inflicted by a wild animal all can be avoided if you take the precaution of keeping your dog in a safe enclosure where he will be protected from such dangers. Don't let your dog run loose; he is likely to stray from home and get into all sorts of trouble.

Many cities and towns now have ordinances that apply to keeping dogs as pets, and in a number of these municipalities there are animal control officials or dog wardens whose job it is to enforce these regulations. In fact, in certain areas there are fines imposed on dog owners who are negligent about controlling their animals. One such familiar regulation involves the curbing of dogs, for sanitary as well as esthetic reasons. In quite a few areas, dog owners are prohibited from allowing their canines, whether leashed or unleashed, to defecate or urinate on someone else's property. There are laws in most places which require dogs to be licensed and inoculated against the dread disease, rabies. Laws, of course, vary from place to place, so save yourself from legal headaches by finding out which rules in your community apply to you as a dog owner. The laws, it should be mentioned, are designed not only to protect the citizenry from acts of canine destruction; they also serve as protection for your dog! So don't wait until your pooch accidentally mauls a young child or scatters the contents of your neighbor's garbage cans or digs holes in carefully cultivated flower beds to exercise your responsibility. Start with a proper attitude as soon as your four-legged companion becomes part of your family.

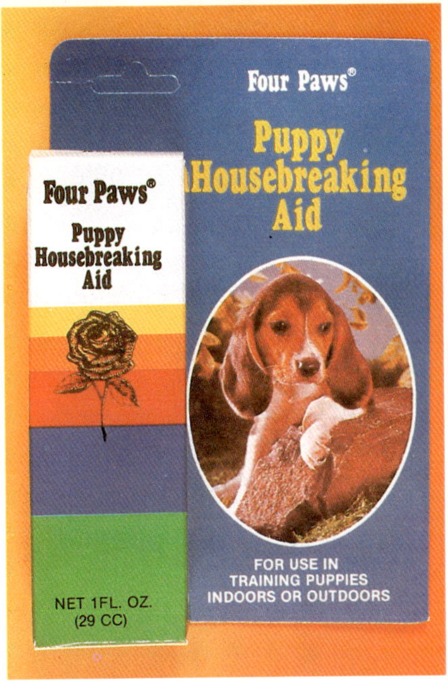

Properly caring for one's dog is a multi-faceted responsibility which can be divided by the various members of the family. Products presently available on the market make the tasks of canine care, the training and maintenance of your dog, remarkably more simple. Responsible and informed dog owners take advantage of a great many of these products, available at pet shops everywhere.

GETTING ACQUAINTED

Plan to bring your new pet home in the morning so that by nightfall he will have had some time to become acquainted with you and his new environment. Avoid introducing the pup to the family around holiday time, since all of the extra excitement will only add to the confusion and frighten him. Let the puppy enter your home on a day when the routine is normal. For those people who work during the week, a Saturday morning is an ideal time to bring the puppy to his new home; this way he has the entire weekend to make adjustments before being left alone for a few hours, come Monday morning.

Let the puppy explore, under your watchful eye of course, and let him come to know his new home without stress and fear.

Resist the temptation to handle him too much during these first few days. And, if there are other dogs or animals around the house, make certain all are properly introduced. If you observe fighting among the animals, or some other problem, you may have to separate all parties until they learn to accept one another. Remember that neglecting your other pets while

Ch. Hoch Haven Maida's Memory enjoys the chance to exercise in the open pasture. Owner-bred by Mr. and Mrs. Haworth F. Hoch, Sweetbriar Farm.

Facing page:
Unlike any breed of dog, the Shetland Sheepdog puppy possesses a particular kind of charm which is disarming and irresistible. These two puppies are fine tribute to this quality.

showering the new puppy with extra attention will only cause animosity and jealousy. Make an effort to pay special attention to the other animals as well.

On that eventful first night, try not to give in and let the puppy sleep with you; otherwise, this could become a difficult habit to break. Let him cry and whimper, even if it means a night of restlessness for the entire family. Some people have had success with putting a doll or a hot water bottle wrapped in a towel in the puppy's bed as a surrogate mother, while others have placed a ticking alarm clock in the bed to simulate the heartbeat of the pup's dam and littermates. Remember that this furry little fellow is used to the warmth and security of his mother and siblings, so the adjustment to sleeping alone will take time. Select a location away from drafts and away from the feeding station for placement of his dog bed. Keep in mind, also, that the bed should be roomy enough for him to stretch out in; as he grows older, you may need to supply a larger one.

Prior to the pup's arrival, set up his room and partition it the way you would to keep an infant out of a particular area. You may want to keep his bed, his feeding station, and his toilet area all in the same room—in separate locations—or you may want to set the feeding station up in your kitchen, perhaps, where meals for all family members are served. Whatever you decide, do it ahead of time so that you will have that much less to worry about when your puppy finally moves in with you.

Above all else, be patient with your puppy as he adjusts to life in his new home. If you purchased a pup that is not housebroken, you will have to spend time with the dog—just as you would with a small child—until he develops proper toilet habits. Even a housebroken puppy may feel nervous in strange new surroundings and have an occasional accident. Praise and encouragement will elicit far better results than punishment or scolding. Remember that your puppy wants nothing more than to please you, thus he is anxious to learn the behavior that is required of him.

Feeding Requirements

Soon after your puppy comes to live with you, he will need to be fed. As mentioned already, ask the seller what foods were offered the youngster and stay with that diet for a while. It is important for the puppy to keep eating and to avoid skipping a meal, so entice him with the food to which he is accustomed. If you prefer to switch to some other brand of dog food, each day begin to add small quantities of the new brand to the usual food offering. Make the portions of the new food progressively larger until the pup is weaned from his former diet.

What should you feed the puppy and how often? His diet is really quite simple and relatively inexpensive to prepare. Puppies need to be fed small portions at frequent intervals, since they are growing and their activity level is high. You must ensure that your pup gains weight steadily; with an adult dog, however, growth slows down and weight must be regulated to prevent obesity and a host of other problems. At one time it was thought that home-cooked meals were the answer, with daily rations of meat,

CANINE DIGESTIVE APPARATUS

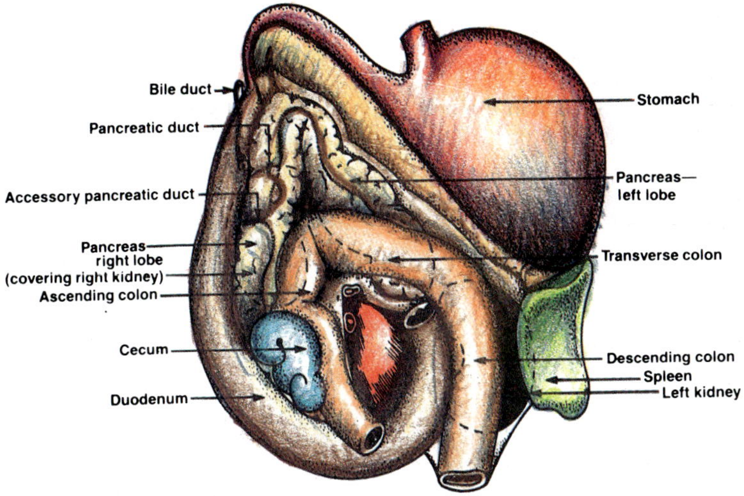

A balanced diet is important to your dog's health, to ensure that the digestive system is in good working order.

vegetables, egg yolk, cereal, cheese, brewer's yeast, and vitamin supplements. With all of the nutritionally complete commercial dog food products readily available, these time-consuming preparations really are unnecessary now. A great deal of money and research has resulted in foods that we can serve our dogs with confidence and pride; and most of these commercial foods have been developed along strict guidelines according to the size, weight, and age of your dog. These products are reasonably priced, easy to find, and convenient to store.

THE PUPPY'S MEALS

After a puppy has been fully weaned from its mother until approximately three months of age, it needs to be fed four times a day. In the morning and evening offer kibble (dog meal) soaked in hot water or broth, to which you have added some canned meat-based food or fresh raw meat cut into small chunks. At noon and bedtime feed him a bit of kibble or whole-grain cereal moistened with milk (moistening, by the way, makes the food easier to digest, since dogs don't typically chew their food). From three to six months, increase the portion size and

The modest but heavenly Sovereign Living Legend, the sire of four champions and many more point winners. Owned by Ariel and Floyd Sleeth, Sovereign Kennels.

Ch. Carmylie Jillian Lauradon with her two pups Ryan and Raini. Jean D. Simmonds, owner.

offer just three meals—one milk and two meat. At six months, two meals are sufficient; at one year, a single meal can be given, supplemented with a few dry biscuits in the morning and evening. During the colder months, especially if your dog is active, you might want to mix in some wheat germ oil or corn oil or bacon drippings with the meal to add extra calories. Remember to keep a bowl of cool, fresh water on hand always to help your dog regulate its body temperature and to aid in digestion.

From one year on, you may continue feeding the mature dog a single meal (in the evening, perhaps, when you have your supper), or you may prefer to divide this meal in two, offering half in the morning and the other half at night. Keep in mind that while puppies require foods in small chunks, or nuggets, older dogs can handle larger pieces of food at mealtime. Discuss your dog's feeding schedule with your veterinarian; he can make suggestions about the right diet for your particular canine friend.

COMPARISON SHOPPING

With so many fine dog-food products on the market today, there is something for everyone's pet. You may want to serve dry food "as is" or mix it with warm water or broth. Perhaps you'll choose to combine dry food with fresh or canned preparations. Some canned foods contain all meat, but they are not complete; others are mixtures of meat and grains, which have been fortified with additional nutrients to make them complete and balanced.

There are also various packaged foods that can be served alone or as supplements and that can be left out for a few hours without spoiling. This self-feeding method, which works well for dogs that are not prone to overweight problems, allows the animal to serve himself whenever he feels hungry. Many people who work during the day find these dry or semi-moist rations convenient to use, and these foods are great to bring along if you travel with your dog.

Be sure to read the labels carefully before you make your dog-food purchases. Most reputable pet-food manufacturers list the

Dogs love canned food, for it is usually more palatable than semi-moist or dry food. Uneaten portions should always be discarded or refrigerated. Never leave them out; otherwise, they will spoil.

There are a number of commercial dog foods on the market. The Iams Company, for example, manufactures foods for both dogs and cats. Check with your local pet shop, grooming salon, or veterinarian for more information—or write to the manufacturer.

For the incalculable amount of love and loyalty your Sheltie provides you, properly taking care of him is but a small price to pay!

ingredients and the nutritional content right on the can or package. Instructions are usually included, besides, so that you will know how much to feed your dog to keep him thriving and in top condition. A varied, well-balanced diet that supplies the proper amounts of protein, carbohydrate, fat, vitamins, minerals, and water is important to keep your puppy healthy and to guarantee its normal development. Adjustments to the diet can be made, under your veterinarian's supervision, according to the individual puppy, his rate of growth, his activity level, and so on. Liquid or powder vitamin and mineral supplements, or those in tablet form, are available and can be given if you need to feel certain that the diet is balanced.

Serve your dog's meals in sturdy dishes that are easy to clean. Photo, Sally Anne Thompson.

DEVELOPING GOOD EATING HABITS

Try to serve your puppy its meals at the same time each day and in the same location so that he will get used to his daily routine and develop good eating habits. A bit of raw egg, cottage cheese, or table scraps (leftover food from your own meals) can be offered from time to time; but never accustom your dog to eating human "junk food." Cake, candy, chocolate, soda, and other snack foods are for people, not dogs. Besides, these foods provide only "empty" calories that your pet doesn't need if he is to stay healthy. Avoid offering spicy, fried, fatty, or starchy foods; rather, offer leftover meats, vegetables, and gravies.

Pet shops stock a wide variety of food and water dishes.

Get in the habit of feeding your puppy or your grown dog his *own* daily meals of dog food. If ever you are in doubt about what foods and how much to serve, consult your veterinarian.

FEEDING GUIDELINES

Some things to bear in mind with regard to your dog's feeding regimen follow:

- Nutritional balance, provided by many commercial dog foods, is vital; avoid feeding a one-sided diet of all-meat. Variety in the kinds of meat

Make certain that the feeding dish you select is one large enough to hold your dog's meal. Photo, Vincent Serbin.

(beef, lamb, chicken, liver) or cereal grains (wheat, oats, corn) that you offer your dog is of secondary importance compared to the balance or "completeness" of dietary components.

- Always refrigerate opened canned food so that it doesn't spoil. Remember to remove all uneaten portions of canned or moistened food from the feeding dish as soon as the pup has finished his meal. Discard the leftover food immediately and thoroughly wash and dry the feeding dish, as dirty dishes are a breeding ground for harmful germs.
- When offering dry foods, always keep a supply of water on hand for your dog. Water should be made available at all times, incidentally, even if dry foods are not left out for self-feeding. Each day the water dish should be washed in soap and hot water, rinsed well, and dried; a refill of clean, fresh water should be provided daily.
- Food and water should be served at room temperature, neither too hot nor too cold, so that it is more palatable for your puppy.
- Serve your pup's meals in sturdy hard-plastic, stainless steel, or earthenware containers, ones that won't tip over as the dog bolts his food down. Some bowls and dishes are weighted to prevent spillage, while others fit neatly into holders which offer support. Feeding dishes should be large enough to hold each meal.

By keeping an automatic waterer available for your dog, you will ensure that he has plenty of water to drink.

- Whenever the nutritional needs of your dog change, that is to say, when it grows old; if it becomes ill, obese, or pregnant; or if it starts to nurse its young, special diets are in order. Always contact your vet for advice on these special dietary requirements.

- Feed your puppy at the same regular intervals each day; reserve treats for special occasions or, perhaps, to reward good behavior during training sessions.
- Hard foods, such as biscuits and dog meal, should be offered regularly. Chewing on these hard, dry morsels helps the dog keep its teeth clean and its gums conditioned.
- Never overfeed your dog. If given the chance, he will accept and relish every in-between-meal tidbit you offer him. This pampering will only put extra weight on your pet and cause him to be unhealthy in the long run.
- Do not encourage your dog to beg for food from the table while you are eating your meals.

RAWHIDE CHEWS FOR DOGS

The most popular material from which dog chews are made is the hide from cows, horses, and other animals. Most of these chews are made in foreign countries where the quality of the hide is not good enough for making leather. These foreign hides may contain lead antibiotics or insecticides which might be detrimental to the health of your dog . . . or even your children. It is not unknown that a small child will start chewing on a piece of rawhide meant for the dog!

Rawhide is flavorful to dogs. They like it. Basically it is good for them to chew on, but dogs think rawhide is food. They do not play with it nor do they use it as a Pooch Pacifier® to relieve doggie tension. They eat it as

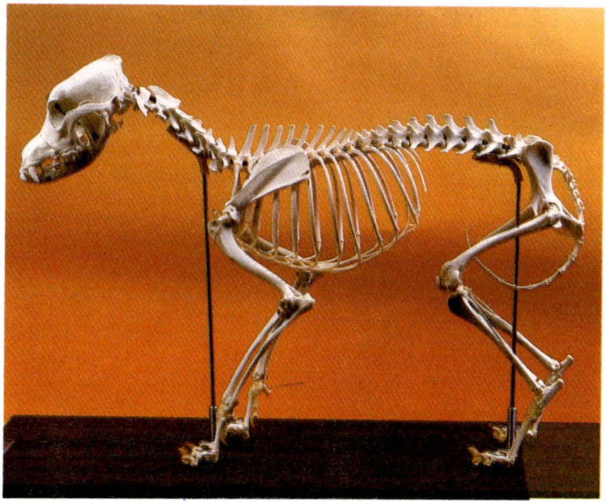

Proper nourishment contributes to good bone development in dogs.

they would any other food. This is dangerous, for the hide is very difficult for dogs to digest and swallow, and many dogs choke on large particles of rawhide that become stuck in their throats. *Before you offer your dog rawhide chews, consult your veterinarian.* Vets have a lot of experience with chewing devices; ask them what they recommend.

permanent teeth through the gums, to assure normal jaw development and to settle the permanent teeth solidly in the jaws.

The adult dog's desire to chew stems from the instinct for tooth cleaning, gum massage, and jaw exercise—plus the need to vent periodic doggie tensions.

Dental caries, as it affects the teeth of humans, is virtually

ALL DOGS NEED TO CHEW

Puppies and young dogs need something with resistance to chew on while their teeth and jaws are developing—for cutting the puppy teeth, to induce growth of the permanent teeth under the puppy teeth, to assist in getting rid of the puppy teeth at the proper time, to help the

Gumabone®, manufactured by the Nylabone® Corporation, is the safest, most economical chew toy that you can give your dog. These flexible bones come in various sizes, depending on the size of your dog.

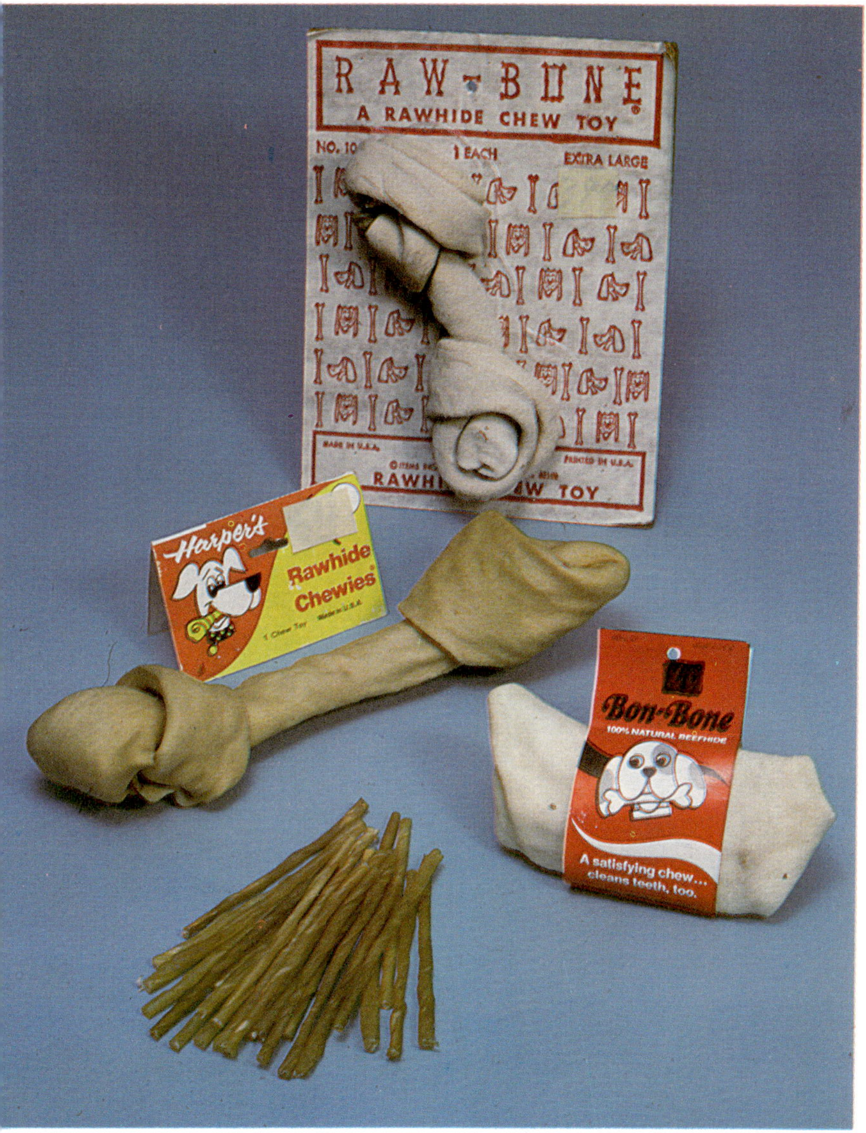

Most pet shops carry high-quality rawhide chews. They are available in many sizes, shapes, and degrees of quality.

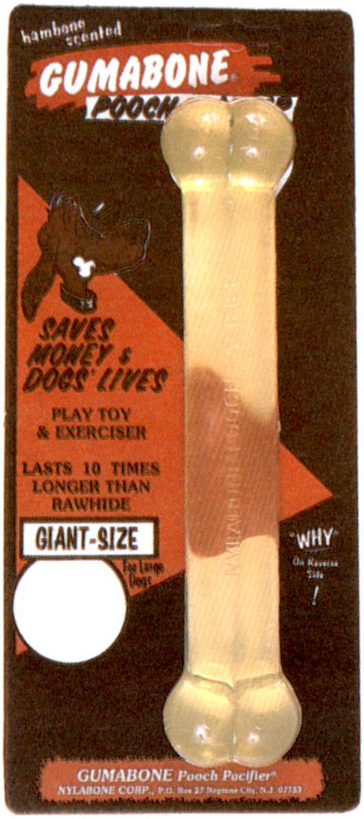

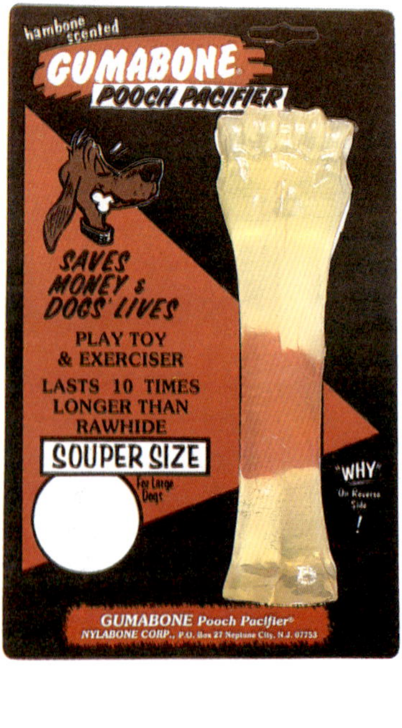

Gumabone®, made of inert soft thermoplastic polymer, was created specifically for dogs whose teeth are too soft for nylon Nylabone® products. There are many advantages that you should know about as a consumer of products for your dog: Gumabone® is practically indestructible and will last 50 times longer than vinyl toys and 10 times longer than rawhide; Gumabone® can be boiled to remove harmful germs; Gumabone® is artificially flavored, ham-scented, and especially appealing to dogs; and Gumabone® comes with a guarantee.

unknown in dogs; but tartar accumulates on the teeth of dogs, particularly at the gum line, more rapidly than on the teeth of humans. These accumulations, if not removed, bring irritation and then infection, which erodes the tooth enamel and ultimately destroys the teeth at the roots.

Tooth and jaw development will normally continue until the dog is more than a year old—but sometimes much longer, depending upon the dog, chewing exercise, the rate at which calcium can be utilized and many other factors, known and unknown, which affect the development of individual dogs. Diseases, like distemper for example, may sometimes arrest development of the teeth and jaws, which may resume months or even years later.

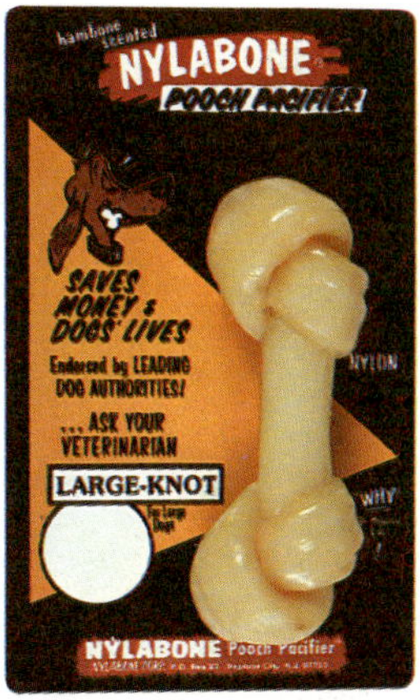

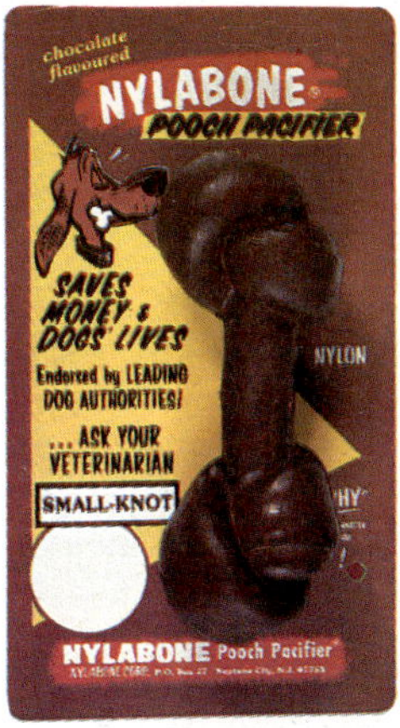

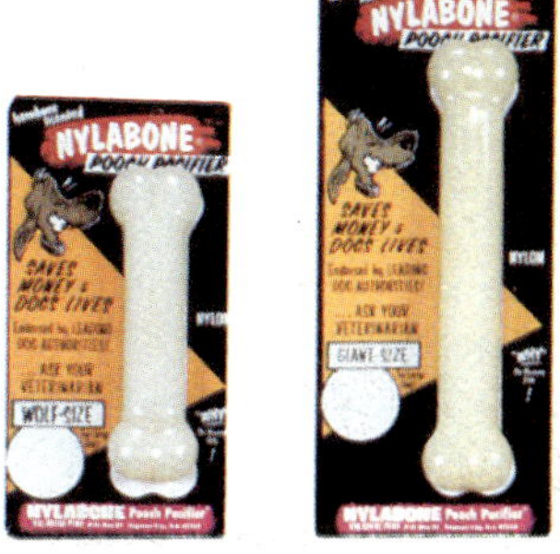

The ever-popular Nylabone® products have been designed as therapeutic devices to vent doggie frustration. These pooch pacifiers® satisfy your dog's need to chew and they aid in tooth and jaw development in puppies. Endorsed by leading dog authorities, Nylabone® products are made for all *dog breeds, no matter what their size or age.*

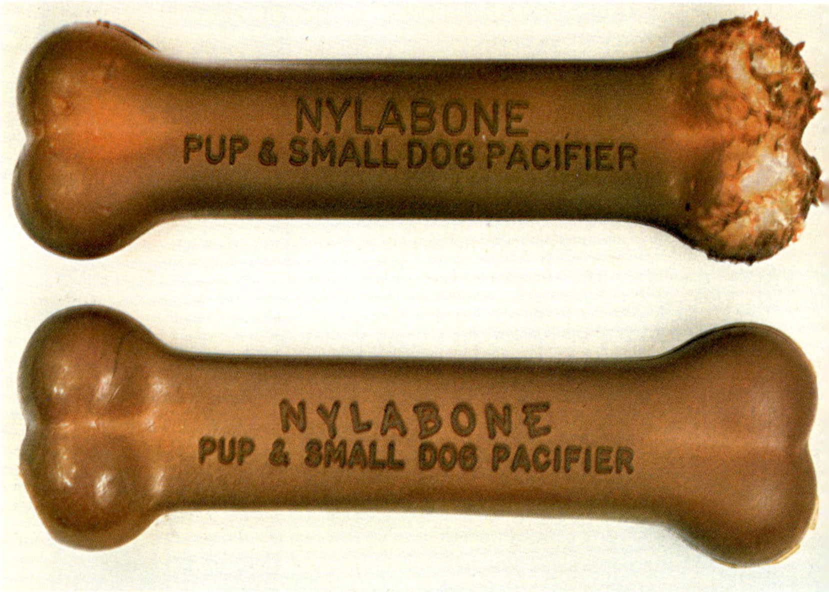

The thin film of chocolate in chocolate Nylabone® products is not on the surface where you can taste or smell it. It's slightly under the surface where it can't be washed off by the dog's saliva. After normal chewing (top), the Nylabone® becomes worn; when this happens, throw it away and purchase a new one.

This is why dogs, especially puppies and young dogs, will often destroy valuable property when their chewing instinct is not diverted from their owner's possessions, particularly during the widely varying critical period for young dogs. Saving your possessions from destruction, assuring proper development of teeth and jaws, providing for "interim" tooth cleaning and gum massage, and channeling doggie tensions into a non-destructive outlet are, therefore, all dependent upon the dog's having something suitable for chewing readily available when his instinct tells him to chew. If your purposes, and those of your dog, are to be accomplished, what you provide for chewing must be desirable from the doggie viewpoint, have the necessary functional qualities, and, above all, be safe for your dog.

It is very important that dogs not be permitted to chew on anything they can break or indigestible things from which they can bite sizeable chunks.

Sharp pieces, such as those from a bone which can be broken by a dog, may pierce the intestine wall and kill. Indigestible things which can be bitten off in chunks, such as toys made of rubber compound or cheap plastic, may cause an intestinal stoppage; if not regurgitated, they are certain to bring painful death unless surgery is promptly performed.

Strong natural bones, such as 4-to 8-inch lengths of round shin bone from mature beef—either the kind you can get from your butcher or one of the varieties available commercially in pet stores—may serve your dog's teething needs, if his mouth is large enough to handle them effectively.

You may be tempted to give your puppy a smaller bone and he may not be able to break it when you do, but puppies grow rapidly and the power of their jaws constantly increases until maturity. This means that a growing dog may break one of the smaller bones at any time, swallow the pieces and die painfully before you realize what is wrong.

Many people have the mistaken notion that their dog's teeth are like those of wild carnivores or of dogs from antiquity. The teeth of wild carnivorous animals and those found in the fossils of the dog-like creatures of antiquity have far thicker and stronger enamel than those of our contemporary dogs.

All hard, natural bones are highly abrasive. If your dog is an avid chewer, natural bones may wear away his teeth prematurely; hence, they then should be taken away from your dog when the teething purposes have been served. The badly worn, and usually painful, teeth of many mature dogs can be traced to excessive chewing on animal bones. Contrary to popular belief, knuckle bones that can be chewed up and swallowed by the dog provide little, if any, useable calcium or other nutriment. They do, however, disturb the digestion of most dogs and might cause them to vomit the nourishing food they really need.

Never give a dog your old shoe to chew on, even if you have removed all the nails or metal parts, such as lace grommets, buckles, metal arches, and so on. Rubber heels are especially dangerous, as the dog can bite off chunks, swallow them, and suffer from intestinal blockage as a result. Additionally, if the rubber should happen to have a nail imbedded in it that you cannot detect, this could pierce or tear the intestinal wall. There is always the possibility, too, that your dog may fail to differentiate between his shoe and yours and chew up a good pair while you're not looking. It is strongly recommended that you refrain from offering old shoes as chew toys since there are much safer products available.

Rawhide products have become very popular. However they don't serve the primary chewing functions very well, they are a bit messy when wet from mouthing, and most dogs chew them up rather rapidly. They have been considered safe for dogs until recently. Now, more and more incidents of death, and near death, by strangulation have been reported to be the result of partially swallowed chunks of rawhide swelling in the throat. Currently, some veterinarians have been attributing cases of acute constipation to large pieces of incompletely digested rawhide in the intestine.

The nylon bones, especially those with natural meat and bone fractions added, are probably the most complete, safe, and economical answer to the chewing need. Dogs cannot break them or bite off sizeable chunks; hence, they are completely safe. And being longer lasting than other things offered for the purpose, they are economical.

Hard chewing raises little bristle-like projections on the surface of the nylon bones to provide effective interim tooth cleaning and vigorous gum massage, much in the same way your tooth brush does it for you. The little projections are raked off and swallowed in the form of thin shavings, but the chemistry of the nylon is such that they break down in the stomach fluids and pass through without effect.

The toughness of the nylon provides the strong chewing resistance needed for important jaw exercise and effective help for the teething functions; however, there is no tooth wear because nylon is non-abrasive.

Make sure that you replace your dog's Gumabone® when the knuckle has worn down, as indicated in this photo.

Being inert, nylon does not support the growth of microorganisms; and it can be washed in soap and water, or it can be sterilized by boiling or in an autoclave.

There are a great variety of Nylabone® products available that veterinarians recommend as safe and healthy for your dog or puppy to chew on. These Nylabone® Pooch Pacifiers® can't splinter, chip, or break off in large chunks; instead, they are

Unfortunately, many nylon chew products have been copied. These inferior quality copies are sold in supermarkets and other chain stores. The really good products are sold only through veterinarians, pet shops, grooming salons and places where the sales people really know something about dogs. The good products have the flavor impregnated *into* the bone. This makes the taste last longer. The smell is undetectable to humans.

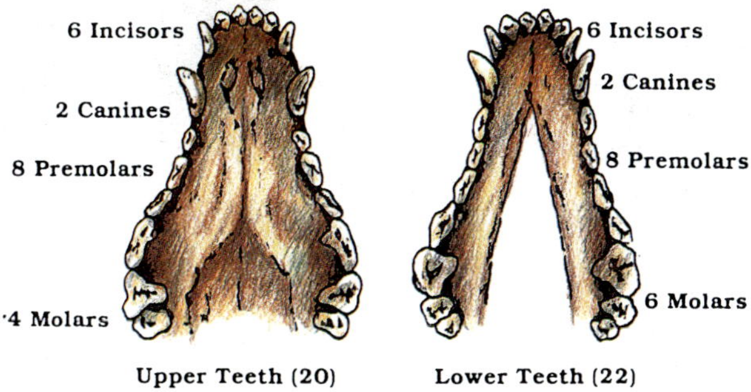

Correct Dentition

frizzled by the dog's chewing action, and this creates a toothbrush-like surface that cleanses the teeth and massages the gums. At the same time, these hard-nylon therapeutic devices channel doggie tension and chewing frustation into constructive rather than destructive behavior.

The artificial bones which have a strong odor are poor-quality bones with the odor sprayed on to impress the dog owner (not the dog)! These heavily scented dog toys may impart the odor to your carpets or furniture if an odor-sprayed bone lies there wet from a dog's chewing on it.

If you want a soft, chewy play

toy, look for Gumabone® products wherever Nylabone® products are sold. These flexible toys are available in various sizes of bones, balls, knots, and rings (and even a tug toy) designed to provide safe entertainment for you and your dog. These great aids for teaching your canine companion how to retrieve are made of a soft, thermoplastic polymer that lasts at least ten times longer than other rawhide, rubber, or vinyl chew toys, making them very economical. If your dog is able to chew apart a Gumabone® toy, although most dogs cannot, it is probably because you gave him a Gumabone® toy that was too small. Replace it with a larger one and most likely he will not be able to chew it apart. These ham-flavored toys will provide scores of hours of fun for most dogs that like chewing on soft items.

Nothing, however, substitutes for periodic professional attention to your dog's teeth and gums, not any more than your toothbrush can do that for you. Have your dog's teeth cleaned by your veterinarian at least once a year—twice a year is better—and he will be healthier, happier, and a far more pleasant companion.

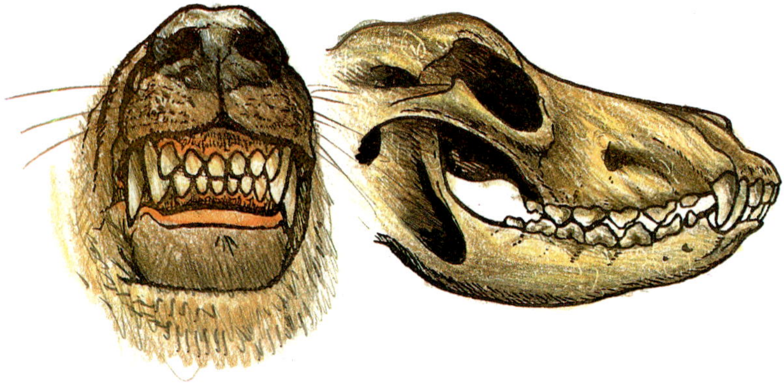

Shown is the scissors bite (seen in most dogs), in which the outer side of the lower incisors touches the inner side of the upper incisors.

Accommodations

Puppies newly weaned from their mother and siblings should be kept warm at all times. As they get older, gradually they can be acclimated to cooler temperatures. When you purchase your dog, find out from the seller whether he is hardy and can withstand the rigors of outdoor living. Many breeds have been known to adapt well to a surprising number of environments, so long as they are given time to adjust. If your pup is to be an indoor companion, perhaps a dog bed in the corner of the family room will suffice, or maybe you'll want to invest in a crate for him to call his "home" whenever he needs to be confined for short intervals. You might plan to partition off a special room, or part of a room, for your pooch; or you may find that a heated garage or finished

Exercise pens are useful whenever you have to confine your dog for short periods—at dog shows, at home, or in motels when you are traveling.

Some dogs like to curl up in their own doggie haven. Check you local pet shop for such items.

basement works well as your dog's living quarters. If your breed can tolerate living outside, you may want to buy or build him his own dog house with an attached run. Or it might be feasible to place his house in your fenced-in backyard. The breed that can live outdoors fares well when he has access to some sort of warm, dry shelter during periods of inclement weather. As you begin thinking about where your canine friend will spend most of his time, you'll want to consider his breed, his age, his temperament, his need for exercise, and the money, space, and resources you have available to house him.

THE DOG BED

In preparing for your puppy's arrival, it is recommended that a dog bed be waiting for him so that he has a place to sleep and rest. If indeed you have provided him with his own bed or basket, ensure that it is in a warm, dry, draft-free spot that is private but at the same time near the center of family activity. Refrain from placing his bed near the feed and water dishes or his toilet area. You may want to give your puppy something with which to snuggle, such as a laundered towel or blanket or an article of old clothing. Some dogs have been known to chew apart their beds and bedding, but you can easily channel this chewing energy into more constructive behavior simply by supplying him with some safe toys or a Nylabone® pacifier for gnawing. Pet shops stock dog beds, among other supplies that you might need for your pup; so select one that is roomy, comfortable, and easy to clean, keeping in mind that you may have to replace the smaller bed with a larger one as the puppy grows to adulthood. Remember to clean and disinfect the bed and sleeping area from time to time, as these can become parasitic playgrounds for fleas, lice, mites, and the like.

If you purchase a wicker dog bed, make sure you outfit it with a nice cushion for your dog's comfort.

THE CRATE

Although many dog lovers may cringe at the mere mention of the word *crate*, thinking of it as a cage or a cruel means of confinement, this handy piece of equipment can be put to good use for puppies and grown dogs alike. Even though you may love your dog to an extraordinary degree, you may not want him to have free rein of the house, particularly when you are not home to supervise him. If used properly, a crate can restrict your dog when it is not convenient to have him underfoot, *i.e.,* when guests are visiting or during your mealtimes.

A surprising number of dog owners who, originally, had negative feelings about crating their dogs, have had great success using them. The crate itself serves as a bed, provided it is furnished with bedding material, or it can be used as an indoor dog house. Not all dogs readily accept crates or being confined in them for short intervals, so for them another means of restriction must be found. But for those dogs that do adjust to spending time in these structures, the crate can be useful in many ways. The animal can be confined for a few hours while you are away from home or at work, or you can bring your crated dog along with you in the car when you travel or go on vacation. They also prove handy as carriers whenever you have to transport a sick dog to the veterinarian.

Most crates are made of sturdy wire or plastic, and some of the collapsible models can be stored conveniently or folded so that they can be moved easily from room to room or from inside the house to the yard on a warm, sunny day. If you allow your puppy or grown dog to become acquainted with its crate by cleverly propping the door open and leaving some of his favorite toys inside, in no time he will come to regard the crate as his own doggie haven. As with a dog bed, place the crate away from drafts in a dry, warm spot; refrain from placing food and water dishes in it, as these only crowd the space and offer opportunity for spillage.

If you need to confine your puppy so that he can't get into

Wire dog crates are indispensable when traveling with your dog. Most fit right on the back seat of your car.

mischief while you're not home, remember to consider the animal's needs at all times. Therefore, select a large crate, one in which the dog can stand up and move around comfortably; in fact, bigger is better in this context. Never leave the animal confined for more than a few hours at a time without letting him out to exercise, play, and, if necessary, relieve himself. Never crate a dog for ten hours, for example, unless you keep the door to the crate open so that he can get out for food and water and to stretch a bit. If long intervals of confinement are necessary, consider placing the unlatched crate in a partitioned section of your house or apartment.

Crates have become the answer for many a dog owner faced with the dilemma of either getting rid of a destructive dog or living with him despite his bad habits. These people who have neither the time nor the patience to train their dogs, or to modify undesirable behavior patterns, can at least restrain their pets during those times they can't be there to supervise. So long as the crate is used in a humane fashion, whereby a dog is confined for no more than a few hours at any one time, it can figure importantly in a dog owner's life. Show dogs, incidentally, learn at an early age that much time will be spent in and out of crates while they are on the show circuit. Many canine celebrities are kept in their crates until they are called to ringside, and they spend many hours crated to and from the shows.

THE DOG HOUSE

These structures, often made of wood, should be made sturdily and offer enough room for your dog to stretch out in when it rests or sleeps. Dog houses that are elevated or situated on a platform protect the animal from cold and dampness that may

If you are not handy with tools and unable to build your pet a dog house, you can purchase one of the many commercially-made ones on the market.

seep through the ground. Of the breeds that are temperature hardy and will live outdoors, some are housed outside during the daytime only; others are permanent outdoor residents day and night, all year 'round.

If your intention is to have a companion that lives out-of-doors, it will be necessary to provide him with a more elaborate house, one that really protects from him the elements. Make sure the dog's house is constructed of waterproof materials. Furnish him with sufficient bedding to burrow into on a chilly night and provide extra insulation to keep out drafts and wet weather. Add a partition (a kind of room divider which separates the entry area from the main sleeping space) inside his house or attach a swinging door to the entrance to help keep him warm when he is inside his residence. The swinging door facilitates entry to and from the dog house, while at the same time it provides protection, particularly from wind and drafts.

Some fortunate owners whose yards are enclosed by high fencing allow their dogs complete freedom within the boundaries of their property. In these situations, a dog can leave its dog house and get all the exercise it wants. Of course such a large space requires more effort to keep clean. An alternative to complete backyard freedom is a dog kennel or run which attaches to or surrounds

This looks like a traditional dog house, only it is not made of wood. It is made of durable plastic

the dog's house. This restricts some forms of movement, such as running, perhaps, but it does provide ample room for walking, climbing, jumping, and stretching. Another option is to fence off part of the yard and place the dog house in the enclosure. If you need to tether your dog to its house, make certain to use a fairly long lead so as not to hamper the animal's need to move and exercise his limbs.

CLEANLINESS

No matter where your dog lives, either in or out of your home, be sure to keep him in surroundings as clean and sanitary as possible. His excrement should be removed and disposed of every day without fail. No dog should be forced to lie in his own feces. If your dog lives in his own house, the floor should be swept occasionally and the bedding should be changed regularly if it becomes soiled. Food and water dishes need to be scrubbed with hot water and detergent and rinsed well to remove all traces of soap. The water dish should be refilled with a supply of fresh water. The dog and his

Never allow your dog to excrete on someone else's property. Always carry a "pooper scooper" with you.

environment must be kept free of parasites (especially fleas and mosquitoes, which can carry disease) with products designed to keep these pests under control. Dog crates need frequent scrubbing, too, as do the floors of kennels and runs. Your pet must be kept clean and comfortable at all times; if you exercise strict sanitary control, you will keep disease and parasite infestation to a minimum.

Your dog needs regular exercise in the form of a brisk walk or a short jog to keep his skeletal structure in good working order.

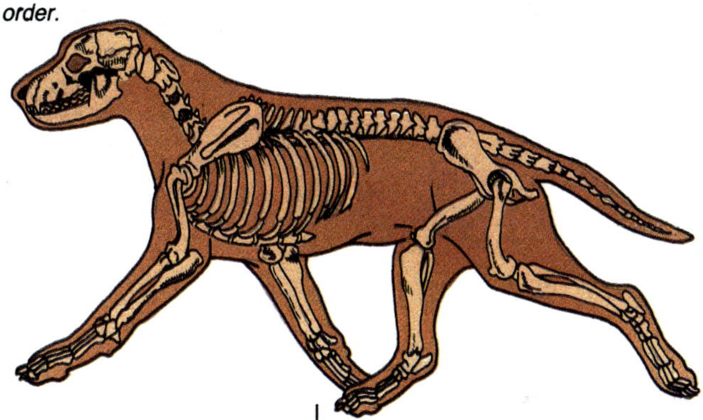

EXERCISE

A well-balanced diet and regular medical attention from a qualified veterinarian are essential in promoting good health for your dog, but so is daily exercise to keep him fit and mentally alert. Dogs that have been confined all day while their owners are at work or school need special attention. There should be some time set aside each day for play—a romp with a family member, perhaps. Not everyone is lucky enough to let his dog run through an open meadow or along a sandy beach, but even a ten-minute walk in the fresh air will do. Dogs that are house-bound, particularly those that live in apartments, need to be walked out-of-doors after each meal so that they can relieve themselves. Owners can make this daily ritual more pleasant both for themselves and their canine companions by combining the walk with a little "roughhousing," that is to say, a bit of fun and togetherness.

Whenever possible, take a stroll to an empty lot, a playground, or a nearby park. Attach a long lead to your dog's collar, and let him run and jump and tone his body through cardiovascular activity. This will help him burn calories and keep him trim, and it will also help relieve tension and stress that may have had a chance to manifest itself while you were away all day. For people who work Monday through Friday, weekend jaunts can be especially beneficial, since there will be more time to spend with your canine friend. You might want to engage him in a simple game of fetch with a stick or a rubber ball. Even such basic tricks as rolling over, standing on the hindlegs, or jumping up (all of which can be done inside the home as well) can provide additional exercise. But if you plan to challenge your dog with a real workout to raise his heart rate, remember not to push him too hard without first warming up with a brisk walk. Don't forget to "cool him down" afterwards with a rhythmic trot until his heart rate returns to normal. Some dog owners jog with their dogs or take them along on bicycle excursions.

At the very least, however, play with your dog every day to keep him in good shape physically and mentally. If you can walk him outdoors, or better yet run with him in a more vigorous activity, by all means do it. Don't neglect

your pet and leave him confined for long periods without attention from you or time for exercise.

Dogs love to chase and catch flying discs, and the Nylabone® Corporation has manufactured several types to please every dog and his owner! Nyladisc® is made of flavored, annealed nylon and features a molded bone on top that makes the disc easier for your dog to pick up. Chocolate Nyladisc® is the chocolate version of Nyladisc®. Gumadisc® is made of soft, flavored annealed polyurethane and also has a molded bone on top for easy retrieval by your dog. Pet shops and veterinarians everywhere endorse these products and can tell you more about them.

EXERCISING FOR YOU AND YOUR DOG

Dogs are like people. They come in three weights: overweight, underweight, and the correct weight. It is fair to say that most dogs are in better shape than most humans who own them. The reason for this is that most dogs accept exercise without objection—people do not! So why not use your dog as an exercise medium for both of you? There are lots of toys at your local pet shop which are designed just for that purpose: to allow you to play and exercise with your dog. Here are a few recommended exercise toys for you and your dog.

Frisbee® Flying Discs*

Who hasn't seen or heard of a Frisbee® flying disc? This flying-saucer–like toy is available in three or more sizes. The small size is 10 cm (4″); the medium size is about 15 cm (6″) and the larger size is 23 cm (9″). The size of the flying disc has little to do with the size of the dog—small puppies chase anything; some larger dogs chase nothing. The advantage of the larger disc is that it is the same size as the toy made for humans only! Start with the size that you think is best suited for your dog. What is much more important is the material from which the flying disc is made; *cheap plastic flying discs are not good for dogs.*

Most people play with cheap polyethylene discs and use these same discs to play with their dogs. Polyethylene plastic discs usually last an hour or so. Every time the dog grabs it, his teeth dig into the cheap plastic, leaving an imprint. In a short while the disc is not useable—and even worse, it may be

If you practice long enough with your dog, you will be amazed at his skill in leaping into the air to retrieve the Nyladisc®. Some dogs can jump as high as 6 feet (2 meters).

Make sure that you do not throw the flying disc where your dog could hurt himself. Play in open spaces, such as a grassy field or a park, where there are no cars or pedestrians.

dangerous, since the dog can break off a chunk and swallow it, or the distorted disc can swerve out of control and hit someone. Polyethylene is hard, too.

Nylon Discs

Your pet shop will have a nylon disc that has a dog bone molded into the top of it. While this may look silly at first, the advantage is simple. When a typical Frisbee® lands on a flat surface, the dog may be unable to grasp it with its mouth or turn it over with its paw. Thus frustrated, the dog loses interest in the game and you will have to fetch it yourself. The nylon disc with the bone molded on top of it allows the dog the option of flipping it over with its paw or grasping it with its mouth. It also has more capacity; thus you can use it as a food or water dish. The nylon disc may also be flavored and scented, besides being annealed, so your dog can find it more easily if it gets lost in the woods or high grass.

Polyurethane Flexible Floppy Flying Discs

The greatest advance in flying discs came with the manufacture of these discs from polyurethane. The polyurethane

Before training your dog to catch and retrieve a flying disc, such as Nyladisc®, learn how to throw it by flicking the wrist.

is so soft that it doesn't hurt you, your dog, or the window it might strike accidentally. Only very, very rarely can it break a window—usually one that was already cracked. The polyurethane Gumadisc® is floppy and soft. It can be folded and fits into your pocket. It is also much tougher than cheap plastics, and most pet shops guarantee that it will last ten times longer than cheap plastic discs.

With most flying discs made for dogs comes an instruction booklet on how to use the disc with your canine friend. Basically, you play with the dog and the disc so the dog knows the disc belongs to him. Then you throw it continuously increasing the distance, so that the dog fetches it and brings it back to you.

The exercise for you comes in when your dog stops fetching it, or when you have a partner. The two of you play catch. You stand as far apart as available space allows—usually 30-35 m (100 feet) is more than enough room. You throw the disc at each other, arousing your dog's interest as he tries to catch it. When the disc is dropped or veers off, the dog grabs it and brings it back (hopefully). Obviously you will have to run to catch the disc before your dog does.

There are contests held all over the world where distance,

height, and other characteristics are measured competitively. Ask your local pet shop to help you locate a Frisbee® Club near you.

*Frisbee® is a trademark of the Kransco Company, California, and is used for their brand of flying disc.

Tug Toys

A tug toy is a hard rubber, cheap plastic, or polyurethane toy which allows a dog and his owner to have a game of tug-o-war. The owner grips one end while the dog grips the other—then they pull. The polyurethane flexible tug toy is the best on the market at the present time. Your pet shop will have one to show you. They are clear in color and stay soft forever. The hard-rubber tug toys get brittle too fast, and they are too stiff for most dogs; however, there *is* a difference in price—just ask the advice of any pet shop operator.

Balls

Nobody has to tell you about playing ball with your dog. The reminder you may need is that you should not throw the ball where traffic might interfere with the dog's catching or fetching of it. The ball should not be cheap plastic (a dog's worst enemy as far as toys are concerned) but made of a substantial material. Balls made of nylon are practically indestructible, but

Before working with your dog, practice throwing the Nyladisc®. Unlike a stick or a ball, the flying disc works on aerodynamic principles, and it takes a bit of skill to get the direction and distance you want.

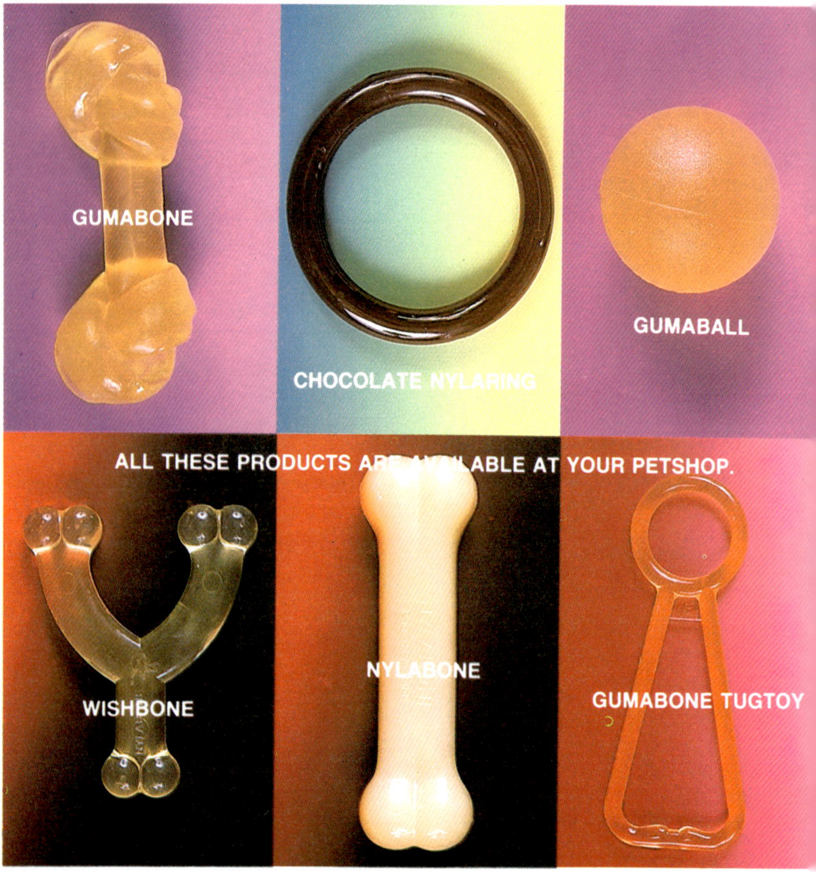

All of these Nylabone® Corporation products are available in pet shops. If a pet shop doesn't have the item you want, they can order it for you. Included in the wide selection of Nylabone® and Gumabone® chew products are knots, rings, balls, wishbones, bones, and tug toys (top). Whenever a chew item wears down (right), it's time to replace it with a new one.

Gumaballs® (above) are soft and chewy and come in several sizes, depending on the size of your dog. The Gumabone® Tug Toy (right) is a great way for you and your dog to have fun together.

they are very hard and must be rolled, never thrown. The same balls made of polyurethane are great—they bounce and are soft. The Nylabone® and Gumabone® balls are scented and flavored, and dogs can easily find them when lost.

Other manufacturers make balls of almost every substance, including plastic, cotton, wood, iron, and steel. Billiard balls, baseballs, tennis balls, and so on, have all been used by dog owners who want their dogs to play with them in a game of catch. A strong caveat is that you use only those balls made especially for dogs.

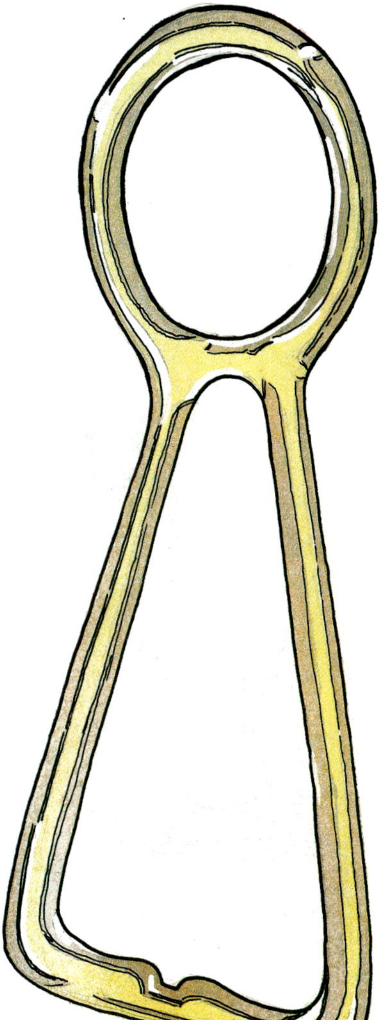

Housebreaking Your Puppy

The new addition to your family may already have received some basic house training before his arrival in your home. If he has not, remember that a puppy will want to relieve himself about half a dozen times a day; it is up to you to specify where and when he should "do his business." Housebreaking is your first training concern and should begin the moment you bring the puppy home.

Ideally, puppies should be taken outdoors after meals, as a full stomach will exert pressure on the bladder and colon. What goes into the dog must eventually come out; the period after his meal is the most natural and appropriate time. When he eliminates, he should be praised and this will increase the likelihood of the same thing happening after every meal. He should also be encouraged to use the same area and will probably be attracted to it after frequent use.

OUTDOOR TRAINING

Some veterinarians have maintained that a puppy could learn to urinate and defecate on command if properly trained. The advantage of this conditioning technique is that your pet would associate the act of elimination with a particular word of your invention rather than with a particular time or place which might not always be convenient or available. So whether you were visiting an unfamiliar place or didn't want to go outside with your dog in sub-zero temperatures, he would still be able to relieve himself when he heard the specific command word. Elimination would occur after this "trigger" phrase or word had set up a conditioned reflex in the dog who would eliminate anything contained in his bladder or bowel upon hearing it. The shorter the word, the more you could repeat it and imprint it on your dog's memory.

Your chosen command word should be given simultaneously with the sphincter opening events in order to achieve perfect and rapid conditioning. This is why it is important initially to familiarize yourself with the tell-tale signs preceding your puppy's elimination process. Then you will be prepared to say the word at the crucial moment. There is usually a sense of urgency on the dog's part; he may follow a sniffing and circling pattern which you will soon recognize. It is important to use the command in his usual area only when you know the puppy can eliminate, i.e., when his stomach or bladder is full. He will soon learn to associate the act with the word. One word of advice, however, if you plan to try out this method: never use the puppy's name or any other word which he might frequently hear about the house—you can imagine the result!

Finally, remember that any training takes time. Such a conditioned response can be obtained with intensive practice with any normal, healthy dog over six weeks of age. Even Pavlov's salivating dogs required fifty repetitions before the desired response was achieved. Patience and persistence will eventually produce results—do not lose heart!

INDOOR TRAINING

Indoors, sheets of newspapers could be used to cover the specific area where your dog should relieve himself. These should be placed some distance away from his sleeping and feeding area, as a puppy will not urinate or defecate where he eats. When the newspapers are changed, the bottom papers should be placed on top of the new ones in order to evoke the purpose of the papers by scent as well as by sight. He should be praised during or immediately after he has made use of this particular part of the room. Each positive reinforcement increases the possibility of his using that area again.

When he arrives, it is advisable to limit the puppy to one room, usually the kitchen, as it most likely has a linoleum or easily washable floor surface. Given the run of the house, the sheer size of the place will seem overwhelming and confusing and he might leave his "signature" on your furniture or clothes! There will be time later to familiarize him gradually with his new surroundings.

Part of housebreaking includes picking up after your dog. There are various housebreaking aids available to do this job.

PATIENCE, PERSISTENCE, AND PRAISE

As with a human baby, you must be patient, tolerant, and understanding of your pet's mistakes, making him feel loved and wanted, not rejected and isolated. You wouldn't hit a baby for soiling his diapers, as you would realize that he was not yet able to control his bowel movements; be as compassionate with your canine infant. Never rub his nose in his excreta. Never indulge in the common practice of punishing him with a rolled-up newspaper. Never hit a puppy with your hand. He will only become "hand-shy" and learn to fear you. Usually the punishment is meted out sometime after the offense so it loses its efficacy anyway as the bewildered dog cannot connect the two events. Moreover, by association, he will soon learn to be afraid of you and anything to do with newspapers—including, perhaps, that area where he is *supposed* to relieve himself!

Most puppies are eager to please; praise, encouragement, and reward (particularly the food variety) will produce far better results than any scolding or physical punishment. Moreover, it is far better to dissuade your puppy from doing certain things, like chewing on chair legs or other furniture, by making those objects particularly distasteful to him. You could smear them with a generous amount of hot chili sauce or cayenne pepper mixed with petroleum jelly, for example. This would make it seem as if the object itself was administering the punishment whenever he attempted to chew it. He probably wouldn't need a second reminder!

Remember that the reason a dog has housebreaking or behavior problems is because his owner has allowed them to develop. This is why you must

A leather harness is a useful piece of equipment to have on hand during training sessions.

begin as you intend to continue, by letting your dog know what is acceptable and unacceptable behavior. It is also important that you be consistent in your demands; you cannot feed him from the dining room table one day and then punish him when he begs for food from your dinner guests.

TRAINING IS NECESSARY

You will want the newest member of your family to be welcomed by everyone; this will not happen if he urinates in every room of the house or barks all night! He needs training in the correct forms of behavior in this new, human world and you cannot expect your puppy to become the perfect pet overnight. He needs your help in his socialization process.

Some puppies learn to relieve themselves outdoors right from the start; others begin with paper training. If you choose the latter, select a particular spot, lay the newspaper, and bring the pup over to his toilet facility whenever he needs to eliminate.

Training greatly facilitates and enhances the relationship of the dog to his owner and to the rest of society. A successfully trained dog can be taken anywhere and behave well with anyone. Indeed, it is that one crucial word—*training*—which can transform an aggressive animal into a peaceful, well-behaved pet. Now, how does this "transformation" take place?

There are all sorts of dog collars available in every color and material imaginable. Nylon web collars, like this one, are especially attractive.

WHEN AND HOW TO TRAIN

Like housebreaking, training should begin as soon as the puppy enters the house. The formal training sessions should be short but frequent, for example, ten to fifteen minute periods three times a day. These are much more effective than long, tiring sessions of half an hour which might soon become boring. You are building your relationship with your puppy during these times so make them as enjoyable as possible. It is a good idea to have these sessions *before* the puppy's meal, not after it when he wouldn't feel like exerting himself; the dog will then associate something pleasurable with his training sessions and look forward to them.

THE COLLAR AND LEASH

Your puppy should become used to a collar and leash as soon as possible. If he is very young, a thin, choke-chain collar could be used, but you will need a larger and heavier one for training when he is a little older. Remember to have his name and address on an identification tag attached to his collar, as you don't want to lose your pet if he

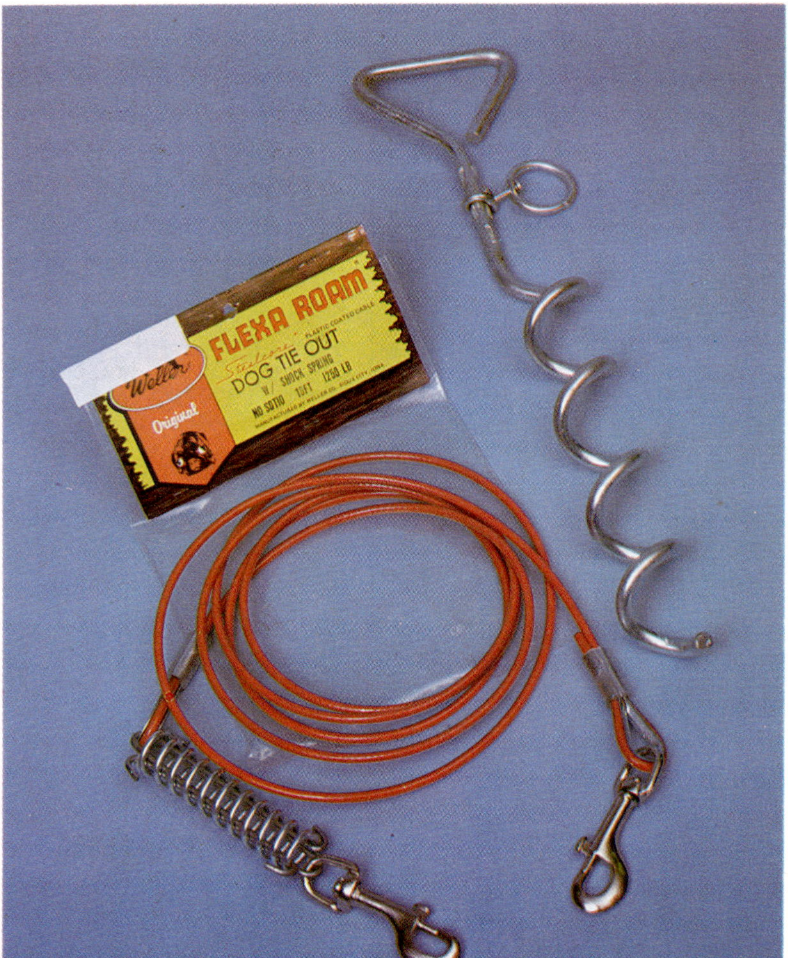

Never let your dog run loose outside; always restrict his ability to roam by tying him to a long leash. The leash can then be fastened to a metal stake. Photo, Vincent Serbin.

should happen to leave your premises and explore the neighborhood!

Let the puppy wear his collar until he is used to how it feels. After a short time he will soon become accustomed to it and you can attach the leash. He might resist your attempts to lead him or simply sit down and refuse to budge. Fight him for a few minutes, tugging on the leash if necessary, then let him relax for the day. He won't be trained until he learns that he must obey the pull under any circumstance, but this will take a few sessions. Remember that a dog's period of concentration is short, so little and often is the wisest course of action—and patience is the password to success.

Some dog owners prefer to use a figure-eight–style harness in conjunction with a leash, as the harness restrains the dog in a way that a simple collar cannot.

A six-foot lead, or leash, is handy if you plan to walk your dog outdoors. It is important to purchase a lead that is strong enough to hold the weight of your dog.

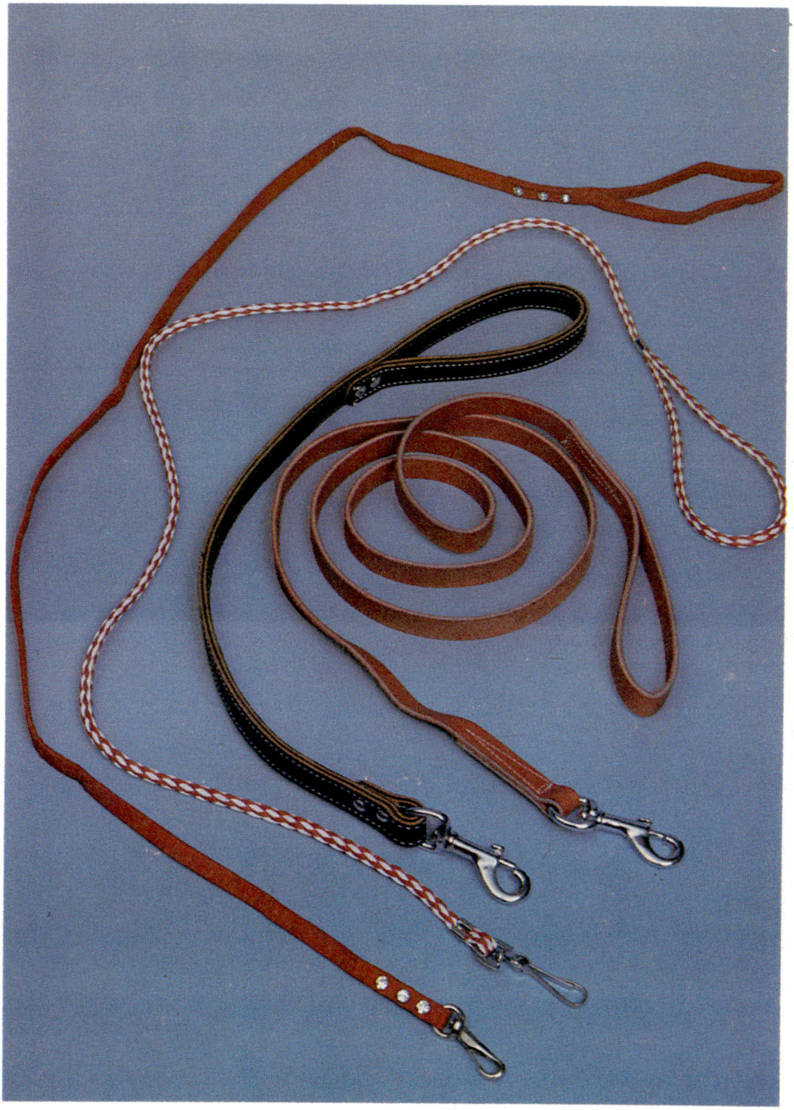

Pet shops stock many different types of dog leads. Photo, Vincent Serbin.

GIVING COMMANDS

When you begin giving your puppy simple commands, make them as short as possible and use the same word with the same meaning at all times, for example, "Heel," "Sit," and "Stay." You must be consistent; otherwise your puppy will become confused. The dog's name should prefix all commands to attract his attention. Do not become impatient with him however many times you have to repeat your command.

A good way to introduce the "Come" command is by calling the puppy when his meal is ready. Once this has been learned, you could call your pet to you at will, always remembering to praise him for his prompt obedience. This "reward" or positive reinforcement is such a crucial part of training that a Director of the New York Academy of Dog Training constructed his whole teaching program upon the methods of "Love, Praise, and Reward." Incidentally, if you use the command "Come," use it every time. Don't switch to "Come here" or "Come boy," as this will only confuse your dog.

It is worth underlining the fact that punishment is an ineffective teaching technique. We have already seen this in housebreaking and, for example, if your pup should run away, it would be senseless to beat him when he eventually returns. He would only connect the punishment with his return, not with the running away! Also, never call him to you to punish him, as he will soon learn not to respond when you call his name.

SOME SPECIFIC COMMANDS

"Sit." This is one of the easiest and most useful commands for your dog to learn, so it is a good idea to begin with it. The only equipment required is a leash, collar, and a few tasty tidbits. Take your dog out for some exercise before his meal. After about five minutes, call him to you, praise him when he arrives, and slip his collar on him. Hold the leash tightly in your right hand; this should force the dog's head up and focus his attention on you. As you say "Sit" in a loud, clear voice, with your left hand press steadily on his rump until he is in a sitting position. As soon as he is in the correct position, praise him and give him the tidbit you have in your hand. Now wait a few minutes to let him rest and repeat the routine. Through repetition, the dog soon associates the word with the act. Never make the lesson too long. Eventually your praise will be reward enough for your puppy.

It is exciting to watch a dog go through his paces at an obedience trial. In order to earn his obedience degrees, a dog must successfully complete various exercises. Photo, Isabelle Francais.

"Sit-Stay/Stay." To teach your pet to remain in one place or "stay" on your command, first of all order him to the sitting position at your side. Lower your left hand with the flat of your palm in front of his nose and your fingers pointing downwards. Hold the leash high and taut behind his head so that he cannot move. Speak the command "Sit-stay" and, as you are giving it, step in front of him. Repeat the command and tighten the leash so the animal cannot follow you. Walk completely around him, repeating the command and keeping him motionless by holding the leash at arm's length above him to check his movement. When he remains in this position for about fifteen seconds, you can begin the second part of the training. You will have to exchange the leash for a nylon cord or rope about twenty to thirty feet long. Repeat the whole routine from the beginning and be ready to prevent any movement towards you with a sharp "Sit-stay." Move around him in ever-widening circles until you are about fifteen feet away from him. If he still remains seated, you can pat yourself on the back! One useful thing to remember is that the dog makes associations with what you say, how you say it, and what you do while you are saying it. Do give this command in a firm, clear tone of voice, perhaps using an admonishing forefinger raised in warning to the dog to "stay."

TEACHING TO "HEEL," "COME" AND "DOWN"

When you walk your dog, you should hold the leash firmly in your right hand. The dog should walk on your left so you have the leash crossing your body. This enables you to have greater control over the dog.

Let your dog lead you for the first few moments so that he fully understands that freedom can be his if he goes about it properly. He knows already that when he wants to go outdoors the leash and collar are necessary, so he has respect for the leash. Now, if while walking he starts to pull in one direction, all you do is *stop walking.* He will walk a few steps and then find that he can't walk any further. He will then turn and look into your face. *This is the crucial point!* Just stand there for a moment and stare right back at him . . . now walk another ten feet and stop again. Again your dog will probably walk out the leash, find he can't go any further, and turn around and look again. If he starts to pull and jerk, then just stand there. After he quiets down, just bend down and comfort him as he may be frightened. Keep up this training until he learns not to outwalk you.

"Heel." Once the puppy obeys the pull of the leash, half of your training is accomplished. "Heeling" is a necessity for a well-behaved dog, so teach him to walk beside you, head even with your knee. Nothing looks sadder than a big dog taking his helpless owner for a walk. It is annoying to passers-by and other dog owners to have a large dog, however friendly, bear down on them and entangle dogs, people, and packages.

To teach your dog, start off walking briskly, saying "Heel" in a firm voice. Pull back with a sharp jerk if he lunges ahead,

One of the exercises that a dog will have to perform at an obedience trial to earn his C.D.X. (Companion Dog Excellent) title is the retrieve over high jump.

and if he lags repeat the command and tug on the leash, not allowing him to drag behind. After the dog has learned to heel at various speeds on leash, you can remove it and practice heeling free, but have it ready to snap on again as soon as he wanders.

By fastening a leash to the ring on this coupler, you can walk two dogs at one time.

"Come." Your dog has already learned to come to you when you call his name. Why? Because you only call him when his food is ready or when you wish to play with him or praise him. Outdoors such a response is more difficult to achieve as he is happily playing by himself or with other dogs. So he must be trained to come to you when he is called. To teach him to come, let him reach the end of a long lead, then give the command, gently pulling him towards you at the same time. As soon as he associates the word *come* with the action of moving towards you, pull only when he does not respond immediately. As he starts to come, move back to make him learn that he must come from a distance as well as when he is close to you. Soon you may be able to practice without a leash, but if he is slow to come or actively disobedient, go to him and pull him toward you, repeating the command. Always remember to reward his successful completion of a task.

This modified choke chain is designed to limit the amount it can tighten around a dog's neck.

"Down." A puppy is naturally affectionate and excitable. However, not everyone likes to have a playful pup pounce on them with muddy paws or enthusiastically jump up to greet them. It is important that your puppy understands the command, "Down," and it should be one of the first lessons you teach.

One successful teaching strategy is to raise your knee and bump the dog in the stomach as he jumps up; you use this maneuver when puppies rush at you and leap at your chest. Or you could take him by his front legs and move him backward across the floor until he loses his balance and falls over. It will take patience and persistence before he gets the message but you will avoid a lot of dirty clothes and irate neighbors if you persevere!

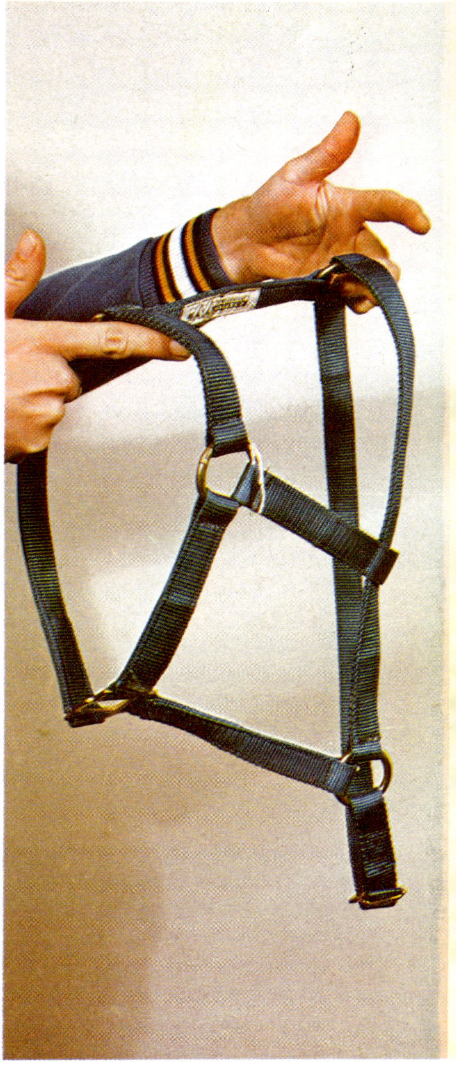

If you are not sure how to place a figure-eight harness on your dog, just ask someone at a pet shop how to do it. Photo, Vincent Serbin.

"Problems with the Barking Dog" and "Aggressive Behavior and Dominance" are extracts from the veterinary monograph *Canine Behavior* (a compilation of columns from *Canine Practice,* a journal published by Veterinary Practice Publishing Company).

PROBLEMS WITH THE BARKING DOG

One of the most frequent complaints about canine behavior is barking. Aside from the biting dog, the barking dog is probably the pet peeve of many non-dog owners. I know of at least one city in which owners of dogs that bark excessively, and for which there are complaints on file, are required to take steps to eliminate the barking.

Canine practitioners are drawn into problems with barking when they are asked for their advice in helping an owner come up with a solution or, as a last resort, when they are requested to perform a debarking operation or even euthanasia. In this column I will deal with some of the factors that apparently cause dogs to bark and suggest some corrective approaches.

Barking is, of course, a natural response for many dogs. They have an inherited predisposition to bark as an alarm when other dogs or people approach their territory. Alarm barking makes many dogs valuable as household watchdogs and is not necessarily undesirable behavior. With a different vocal tone and pattern, dogs bark when they are playing with each other. On occasion dogs have a tendency to bark back at other dogs or join in with other barking dogs.

In addition to inherited barking tendencies, dogs can also learn to bark if the barking is followed, at least sometimes, by a reward. Thus dogs may bark when they wish to come in the house or to get out of a kennel. Some dogs are trained to bark upon hearing the command "speak" for a food reward.

One of the first approaches to take when discussing a barking problem is to determine if the behavior is a manifestation of a natural (inherited) tendency or is learned behavior which has been rewarded in the past.

Can Barking Be Extinguished? Extinction, as a way of eliminating a behavioral problem, may be considered when it is clear that the behavior has been learned and when one can identify the specific rewarding or reinforcing factors that maintain the behavior.

For example, the dog that barks upon hearing the command "speak" is periodically rewarded with food and praise. If a dog is never, ever given food or praise again when it barks after being told to "speak," it will eventually stop this type of barking. This is the process of extinction and it implies that the behavior must be repeated but never again rewarded.

A more practical example of the possible use of extinction would be in dealing with the dog that apparently barks because, at least occasionally, it is allowed in the house. By not allowing the dog in the house until the barking has become very frequent and loud, the owners may have shaped the barking behavior to that which is the most objectionable. If the dog is never allowed in the house again when barking, the barking should eventually be extinguished—at least theoretically.

How Should Punishment Be Used? Sometimes it is not feasible to attempt to extinguish barking even if it seems to be the case that the behavior was learned. This brings up the advisability of punishment. Clients who seek advice in dealing with a barking problem may already have employed some type of punishment such as shouting at the dog or throwing something at it. That this type of punishment is ineffective is attested to by the fact that the client is seeking advice. By shouting at a dog or hitting, a person interferes with what effect the punishment may have on the behavior itself through the arousal of autonomic reactions and escape attempts or submissive responses by the dog.

The Water Bucket Approach
am rather impressed by the ingenuity of some dog owners in coming up with ways to punish a dog for barking without being directly involved in administering the punishment. One such harried dog owner I talked to, who was also a veterinarian, was plagued by his dog barking in the kennel commencing at about 1:30 a.m. every night. A platform to hold a bucket of water was constructed over the area of the kennel in which the dog usually chose to bark. Through a system of hinges, ropes, and pulleys, a mechanism was devised so that the dog owner could pull a rope from his bedroom window, dumping a bucket of water on the dog when he started to bark. The bucket was suspended such that once it was dumped, it uprighted itself and the owner could fill it again remotely by turning on a garden hose. After two appropriate dunkings, the dog's barking behavior was apparently eliminated.

In advising a client on the type of punishment discussed above, keep in mind one important consideration. From the time the owner is ready to administer punishment for barking, every attempt should be made to punish all undesirable barking from that point on and to not allow excessively long periods of barking to go unpunished. Thus it may be necessary to keep a dog indoors when away unless the dog will be punished for barking when the owner is gone.

Alternative Responses Barking dogs are, and probably always will be, one of the enduring problems of dog owners. Barking is relatively effortless, and it is such a natural response for many dogs that it is admittedly hard to eliminate with either punishment or a program of conditioning non-barking. In some instances it may be advisable to forget about eliminating barking and suggest that the problem be dealt with by changing the circumstances which lead to barking. For example, a dog that barks continuously in the backyard while the owners are away may not bark if left in the house while they are gone. But the problem of keeping the dog in the house may be related to inadequate house training or because the dog is shedding hair or climbs onto the furniture. It may be easier to correct these latter behavioral problems than it is to change the barking behavior.

AGGRESSIVE BEHAVIOR AND DOMINANCE

Aggressiveness can have many causes. Determining what kind of aggression an animal is manifesting is a prerequisite to successful treatment of the behavior. A frequent problem that is presented to the practitioner is one of aggression related to dominance.

Dogs, which are social animals, have a hierarchal system of dominance within their pack. This predisposition to take a dominant or submissive position relative to fellow canines also occurs in relationship to people. Only in unusual situations would a submissive dog threaten a dominant animal, and almost never would it physically assault its superior. The dominant dog, however, frequently threatens submissive individuals to maintain its position. In a household setting a person may be the object of threats and when the person backs off, the dog's position is reassured. The aggressive behavior is also reinforced, and when behavior is reinforced it is likely to recur.

Case History The following is a typical case history of a dog presented for aggression stemming from dominance. Max was a two-year-old intact male Cocker Spaniel. He had been acquired by Mr. Smith, one year prior to his owner's marriage, as a puppy. He liked and was well liked by both Mr. and Mrs. Smith. He frequently solicited and received attention from both people. However, several times over the last few months, Max had snapped at Mrs. Smith and repeatedly growled at her. A detailed anamnesis revealed that such incidents usually occurred in situations where the dog wanted his own way or did not want to be bothered. He would growl if asked to move off a chair or if persistently commanded to do a specific task. He growled if Mrs. Smith came between him and a young female Cocker Spaniel acquired a year ago. He also refused to let Mrs. Smith take anything from his possession. Max never showed any of these aggressive behaviors toward Mr. Smith or strangers. Admittedly he did not have much opportunity to demonstrate such behaviors toward strangers. A description of the dog's body and facial postures and circumstances under which the aggression occurred did not indicate that this was a case of fear-induced aggression, but rather one of assertion of dominance.

Mrs. Smith's reaction to the aggression was always to retreat, and, hence, the dog was rewarded for his assertiveness. She had never physically disciplined the dog and was afraid to do so. To encourage her to physically take control of the dog would likely have resulted in her being bitten. The dominance-submissive relationship had to be reversed in a more subtle manner.

Instructions to Client Mrs. Smith was instructed to avoid all situations which might evoke any aggressive signs from Max. This was to prevent any further reinforcement of his growling and threats.

Both she and her husband were not to indiscriminately pet or show affection towards the dog. For the time being if Max solicited attention from Mr. Smith, he was to ignore the dog. Mrs. Smith was to take advantage of Max's desire for attention by giving him a command which he had to obey before she praised and petted him. She was also to take advantage of high motivation levels for other activities whenever such situations arose. Max had to obey a command before she gave him anything—before she petted him, before she let him out or in, etc.

Mrs. Smith also was to assume total care of the dog and become "the source of all good things in life" for Max. She was to feed him, take him on walks, play with him, etc.

Mrs. Smith also spent 5-10 minutes a day teaching Max simple parlor tricks and obedience responses for coveted food rewards as well as praise. These were entirely fun and play sessions—but within a few days the dog had acquired the habit of quickly responding to commands. And this habit transferred over to the non-game situations.

Results Within a few weeks, Max had ceased to growl and threaten Mrs. Smith in situations that he previously had. He would move out of her way or lie quietly when she would pass by him. She could order him off the furniture and handle the female Cocker Spaniel without eliciting threats from Max.

Mrs. Smith still felt that she would not be able to take the objects from Max's possession. Additional instructions were given to her. She then began placing a series of objects at progressively closer distances to the dog while the dog was in a sit-stay position. After she placed the object on the floor for a short time, she would pick it up. If the dog was still in a sit-stay (which it always was), he received a reward of cheese and verbal praise. Eventually the objects were to be placed and removed from directly in front of the dog. At first she was to use objects that the dog did not care much about and then progressively use more coveted items. This was what she was supposed to do, but before she actually had completed the program she called in excitedly to report that she had taken a piece of stolen food and a household ornament from Max's mouth. And he didn't even object! She said she had calmly told Max to sit. He did. He was so used to doing so, in the game and other situations, that the response was now automatic. She walked over, removed the item from his mouth, and praised him.

Mrs. Smith did resume the systematic presentation of objects and put the dog on an intermittent schedule of food and praise reinforcement during the practice sessions. Mr. Smith again began interacting with Max.

A progress check six months later indicated Max was still an obedient dog and had definitely assumed a submissive position relative to both of his owners. The dominance hierarchy between Max and Mrs. Smith had been reversed *without resorting to any physical punishment.* Mrs. Smith was instructed to reinforce her dominance position by frequently giving Max a command and reinforcing him for the appropriate response.

Summary The essential elements in treatment of such cases are as follows. First, of course, there must be a correct diagnosis of what kind of aggressive behavior is occurring. During the course of treatment, the submissive person(s) should avoid all situations that might evoke an aggressive attitude by the dog. All other family members should totally ignore the dog during the treatment interim. The person most dominated by the dog should take over complete care of the dog in addition to spending 5-10 minutes a day teaching the dog tricks or simple obedience commands (sit-stay is a useful one to gain control of the dog in subsequent circumstances). These should be fun-and-games situations. Food rewards are highly recommended in addition to simple praise.

The person submissive to the dog should take the opportunity to give the dog a command, which must be obeyed, before doing anything pleasant for the dog.

It must be emphasized to the owner that no guarantee can be made that the dog will never threaten or be aggressive again. What is being done, as with all other aggression cases, is an attempt to reduce the likelihood, incidence, and intensity of occurrence of the aggressive behavior.

DESTRUCTIVE TENDENCIES

It is ironical but true that a dog's destructive behavior in the home may be proof of his love for his owner. He may be trying to get more attention from his owner or, in other cases, may be expressing his frustration at his owner's absence. An abundance of unused energy may also contribute to a dog's destructive behavior and therefore the owner should ensure that his dog has, at least, twenty minutes of vigorous exercise a day.

As a dog's destructive tendencies may stem from his desire to get more attention from his owner, the latter should devote specific periods each day to his dog when he is actively interacting with him. Such a period should contain practice obedience techniques during which the owner can reward the dog with his favorite food as well as praise and affection.

Planned departure conditioning is one specific technique which has been used to solve the problem of destructive tendencies in a puppy. It eventually ensures the dog's good behavior during the owner's absence. A series of short departures, which are identical to real departures, should condition the dog to behave well in the owner's absence. How is this to be achieved? Initially, the departures are so short (2-5 minutes) that the dog has no opportunity to be destructive. The dog is always rewarded for having been good when the owner returns. Gradually the duration of the departures is increased. The departure time is also varied so that the dog does not know when the owner is going to return. Since a different kind of behavior is now expected, it is best if a new stimulus or "atmosphere" is introduced into the training sessions to permit the dog to distinguish these departures as different from previous departures when he was destructive.

This new stimulus could be the sound of the radio or television. The association which the dog will develop is that whenever the "signal" or "stimulus" is on, the owner will return in an unknown period of time and, if the dog has not been destructive, he will be rewarded. As with the daily owner-dog interaction, the food reward is especially useful.

If the dog misbehaves during his owner's absence, the owner should speak sternly to him and isolate him from social contact for at least thirty minutes. Puppies hate to be ignored. Then the owner should conduct another departure of a shorter time and generously reward good behavior when he returns. The owner should progress slowly enough in the program so that once the departure has been initiated, the dog is never given an opportunity to make a mistake.

If planned departures are working satisfactorily, the departure time may gradually be extended to several hours. To reduce the dog's anxiety when left alone, he should be given a "safety valve" such as the indestructible Nylabone® to play with and chew on.

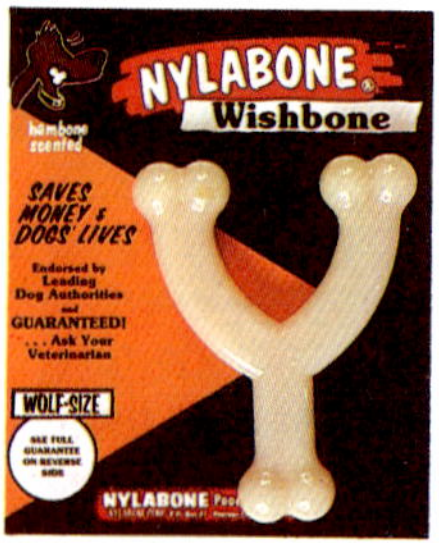

Lucky is the dog who gets a Nylabone® wishbone to chew on! These come in several sizes, including petite (for small dogs), regular (for medium-sized dogs), and wolf (for large or giant breeds).

From the moment you purchase your puppy, the most important person in both your lives becomes your veterinarian. His professional advice and treatment will ensure the good health of your pet and he is the first person to call when illness or accidents occur. Do *not* try to be your own veterinarian or apply human remedies to canine diseases.

However, just as you would keep a first aid kit handy for minor injuries sustained by members of your family at home, so you should keep a similar kit prepared for your pet. First aid for your dog would consist of stopping any bleeding, cleaning the wound, and preventing infection. Thus your kit might contain medicated powder, gauze bandages, and adhesive tape to be used in case of cuts. If the cut is deep and bleeding profusely, the bandage should be applied very tightly to help in the formation of a clot. A tight bandage should not be kept in place longer than necessary, so take your pet to the veterinarian immediately.

Walking or running on a cut pad prevents the cut from healing. Proper suturing of the cut and regular changing of the bandages should have your pet's wound healed in a week to ten days. A minor cut should be covered with a light bandage, for you want as much air as possible to reach the wound. Do not apply wads of cotton to a wound as they will stick to the area and may cause contamination.

You should also keep some hydrogen peroxide available as it is useful in cleaning wounds and is also one of the best and simplest emetics known. Cotton applicator swabs are useful for

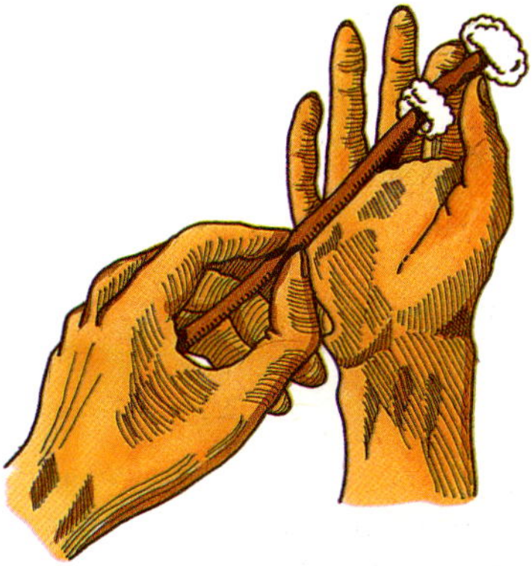

Only your veterinarian should treat an abscess. First he will dip cotton in an antiseptic solution.

applying ointment or removing debris from the eyes. A pair of tweezers should also be kept handy for removing foreign bodies from the dog's throat or body.

Nearly everything a dog might contract in the way of sickness has basically the same set of symptoms: loss of appetite, diarrhea, dull eyes, dull coat, warm and/or runny nose, and a high temperature. Therefore, it is most important to take his temperature at the first sign of illness. To do this, you will need a rectal thermometer which should be lubricated with petroleum jelly. Carefully insert it into the rectum, holding it in place for at least two minutes. It must be held firmly; otherwise there is the danger of its being sucked up into the rectum, or slipping out, thus giving an inaccurate reading. The normal temperature for a dog is between 101° and 102.5°F. If your pet is seriously ill or injured in an accident, your veterinarian will advise you what to do before he arrives.

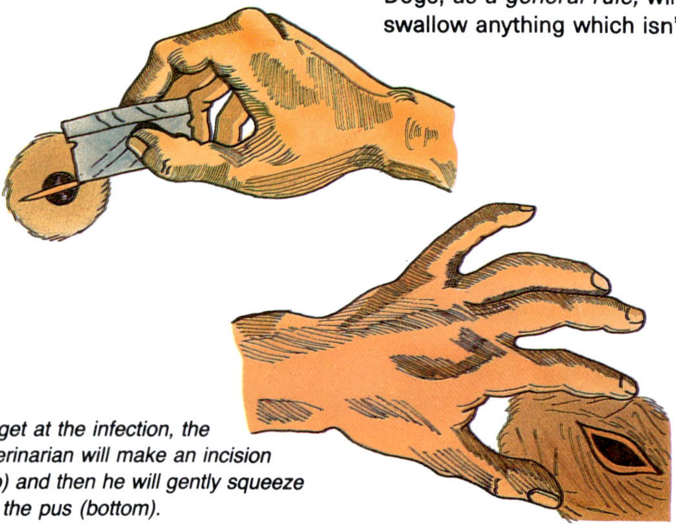

To get at the infection, the veterinarian will make an incision (top) and then he will gently squeeze out the pus (bottom).

SWALLOWING FOREIGN OBJECTS

Most of us have had experience with a child swallowing a foreign object. Usually it is a small coin; occasionally it may be a fruit pit or something more dangerous. Dogs, *as a general rule,* will not swallow anything which isn't edible. There are, however, many dogs that swallow pebbles or small shiny objects such as pins, coins, and bits of cloth and plastic. This is especially true of dogs that are offered so-called "chew toys."

Chew toys are available in many sizes, shapes, colors (dogs are color blind, by the way), and materials. Some even have whistles which sound when the dog's owner plays with it or when the dog chomps on it quickly. Most dogs attack the whistle first, doing everything possible to make it stop squeaking. Obviously, if the whistle is made of metal, a dog can injure its mouth, teeth, or tongue. Therefore, *never* buy a "squeak toy" made with a metal whistle.

Other chew toys are made of vinyl, a cheap plastic which is soft to the touch and pliable. Most of the cute little toys that

Very inexpensive dog toys, usually found in supermarkets and other low-price venues, may be made of polyethylene. These are to be avoided completely, as this cheap plastic is, for some odd reason, attractive to dogs. Dogs destroy the toy in minutes and sometimes swallow the indigestible bits and pieces that come off. Most pet shops carry only safe toys.

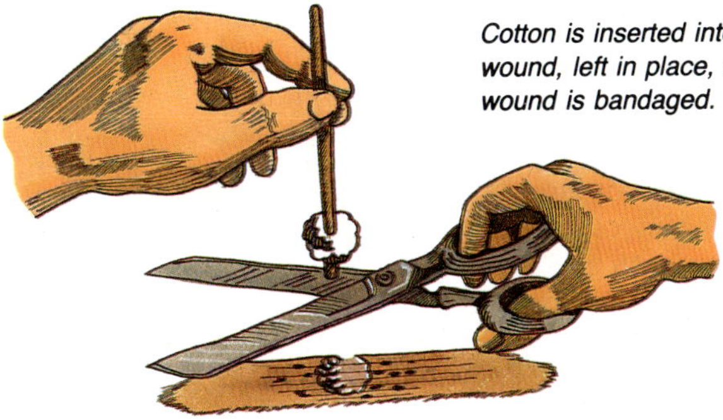

Cotton is inserted into the cleansed wound, left in place, and then the wound is bandaged.

are figures of animals or people are made of this cheap plastic. They are sometimes hand-painted in countries where the cost of such labor is low. Not only is the paint used dangerous to dogs, because of the lead content, but the vinyl tears easily and is usually destroyed by the dog during the first hour. Small bits of vinyl may be ingested and cause blockage of the intestines. You are, therefore, reminded of these things before you buy anything vinyl for your dog!

WHAT TOYS ARE SAFE FOR DOGS?

Hard Rubber Toys made of hard rubber are usually safe for dogs, providing the toy is made of 100% hard rubber and not a compound of rubber and other materials. The rubber must be "virgin" and not re-ground from old tires, tubes, and other scrap rubber products. The main problem with rubber, even 100% virgin rubber, is that it oxidizes quickly, especially when subjected to the ultraviolet rays of the sun and a dog's saliva. The rubber then tends to be brittle, to crack, to dust off, and to be extremely dangerous to dogs that like swallowing things.

Nylon Toys Toys made of nylon could well be the safest of all toys, *providing the nylon is annealed.* Nylon that is not annealed is very fragile and if you smash it against the ground (a hard surface), it might shatter like glass. The same is true when the weather is cold and the nylon drops below freezing. Thus far there is only one line of dog toys that is made of annealed virgin nylon—Nylabone®. These toys are not only annealed but they are flavored and scented. The flavors and scents, such as hambone, are undetectable by humans, but dogs seem to find them attractive.

Some nylon bones have the flavor sprayed on them or molded into them. These cheaper bones are easy to detect—just smell them. If you discern an odor, you know they are poorly made. The main problem with the nylon toys that have an odor is that they are not annealed and they "smell up" the house or car. The dog's saliva dilutes the odor of the bone, and when he drops it on your rug, this odor attaches itself to the rug and is quite difficult to remove.

Annealed nylon may be the best there is but it is not 100% safe. The Nylabone® dog chews are really meant to be Pooch Pacifiers®. This trade name indicates the role intended for the dog, which is to relieve the tension in your excited puppy or adult dog who is left alone or wants to "spite" you. Instead of chewing up the furniture or some other object, he chews up his Nylabone® instead. Many dogs ignore the Nylabone® for weeks, suddenly attacking it when they have to relieve their doggie tensions.

Some dogs may have jaws strong enough to chomp off a piece of Nylabone®, but this is extremely rare. *one word of caution:* the Nylabone® should be replaced when the dog has chewed down the knuckle. Most dogs slowly scrape off small slivers of nylon which pass harmlessly through their digestive tract. The resultant frizzled bone actually becomes a toothbrush.

One of the great characteristics of nylon bones is that they can be boiled and sterilized. If a dog loses interest in his Nylabone®, or it is too hard for him to chew due to his age and the condition of his teeth, you can cook it in some chicken or beef broth, allowing it to boil for 30 minutes. Let it cool down normally. It will then be perfectly sterile and re-flavored for the next dog. *Don't try this with plastic bones, as they will melt and ruin your pot.*

Polyurethane Toys Toys made of polyurethane are almost as good as nylon bones—but not quite. There are several brands on the market: ignore the ones which have scents that you can discern. Some of the scented polyurethane bones have an unbearable odor after it has rubbed off the bone and onto your rug or car seat. Again, look for the better-quality polyurethane toy. Gumabone® is a flexible material, the same as used for making artificial hearts and the bumpers on automobiles, thus it is strong and stable. It is not as strong as Nylabone®, but more dogs like it because it is soft.

The most popular of the Gumabone® toys made in polyurethane are the tug toys, balls, and Frisbee® flying discs. These items are almost clear in color, have the decided advantage of lasting a long time, and are useful in providing exercise for both a dog and his master or mistress.

Whatever dog toy you buy, be sure it is high quality. Pet shops, as a rule, carry the better-quality toys, while supermarkets seem to be concerned only with price. Of course there may be exceptions, but you are best advised to ask your local pet shop operator—or even your veterinarian—what toys are suitable for *your* dog.

In conclusion, if your dog is a swallower of foreign objects,

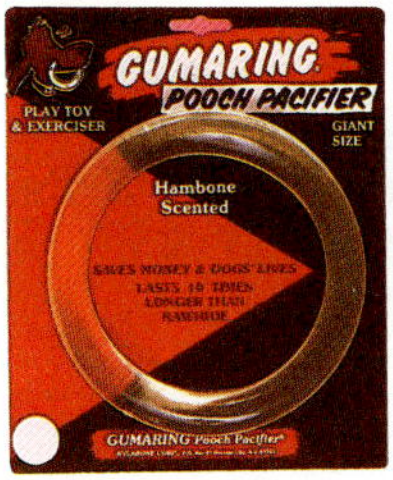

Gumabones® are flexible play toys with which you and your canine companion can have fun. There are Gumarings®, Gumaknots®, and bones in assorted sizes—safe to use, long-lasting, and available at pet shops everywhere.

don't give him anything cheap to chew on. If he swallows a coin, you can hardly blame the Treasury! Unless your dog is carefully supervised, use only the largest size Nylabone®, and replace it as quickly as the dog chews down the knuckles. *Do not let the dog take the Nylabone® outdoors.* First of all he can hide and bury it, digging it up when his tensions rise. Then, too, all nylon becomes more brittle when it freezes, even Nylabone®.

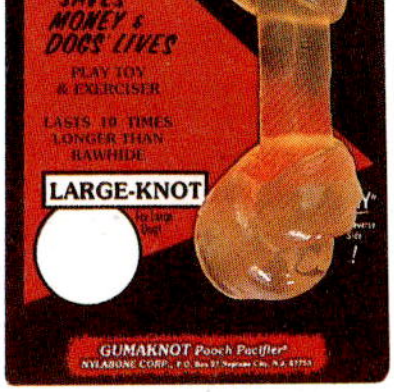

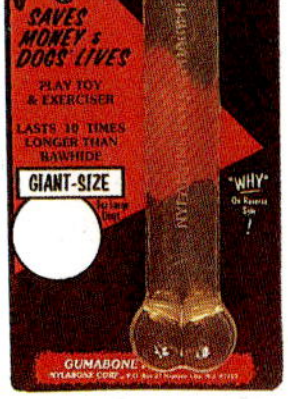

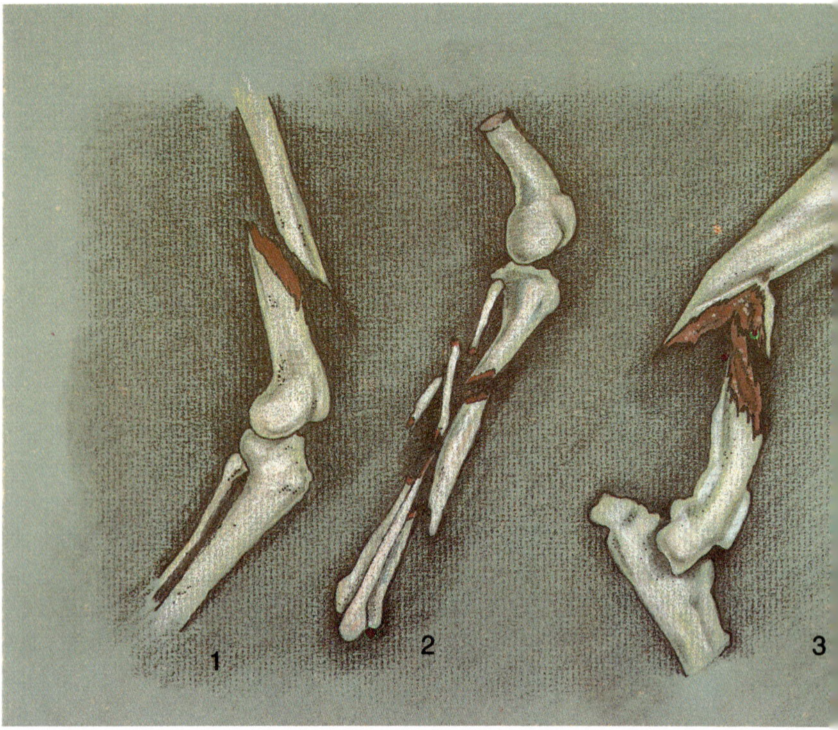

Bone fractures, including I—simple (bones don't penetrate the skin) 2—comminuted (small fragments) 3—compound (bone protrudes through the skin) 4—greenstick and 5—broken ball of femur. All of these, no matter how minor, should be attended to by a veterinarian.

IF YOUR PET SWALLOWS POISON

A poisoned dog must be treated instantly; any delay could cause his death. Different poisons act in different ways and require different treatments. If you know the dog has swallowed an acid, alkali, gasoline, or kerosene, do not induce vomiting. Give milk to dilute the poison and rush him to the vet. If you can find the bottle or container of poison, check the label to see if there is a recommended antidote. If not, try to induce vomiting by giving him a mixture of hydrogen peroxide and water. Mix the regular drugstore strength of hydrogen peroxide (3%) with an equal part of water but do not attempt to pour it down your dog's throat as that could cause inhalation pneumonia. Instead,

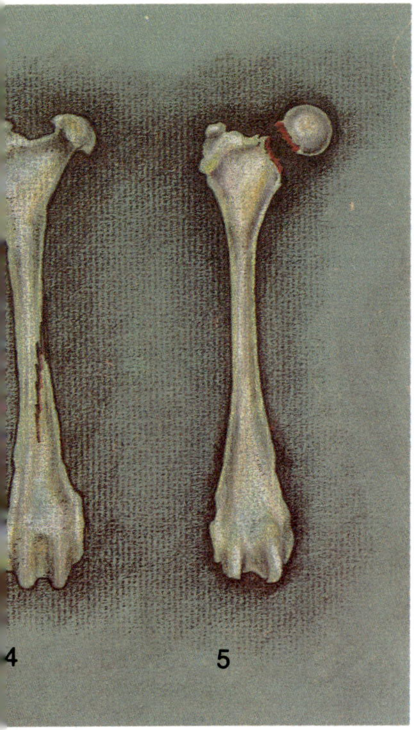

simply pull the dog's lips away from the side of his mouth, making a pocket for depositing the liquid. Use at least a tablespoonful of the mixture for every ten pounds of your dog's weight. He will vomit in about two minutes. When his stomach has settled, give him a teaspoonful of Epsom salts in a little water to empty the intestine quickly. The hydrogen peroxide, on ingestion, becomes oxygen and water and is harmless to your dog; it is the best antidote for phosphorus, which is often used in rat poisons. After you have administered this emergency treatment to your pet and his stomach and bowels have been emptied, rush him to your veterinarian for further care.

DANGER IN THE HOME

There are numerous household products that can prove fatal if ingested by your pet. These include rat poison, antifreeze, boric acid, hand soap, detergents, insecticides, mothballs, household cleansers, bleaches, de-icers, polishes and disinfectants, paints and varnish removers, acetone, turpentine, and even health and beauty aids if ingested in large enough quantities. A word to the wise should be sufficient: what you would keep locked away from your two-year-old child, also keep hidden from your pet.

There is another area where danger lurks within the home and that is among the household plants, which are almost all poisonous, even if swallowed in small quantities. There are hundreds of poisonous plants in the United States, among which are: ivy leaves, cyclamen, lily of the valley, rhododendrons, tulip bulbs, azalea, wisteria, poinsettia leaves, mistletoe, daffodils, delphiniums, foxglove leaves, the jimson weed—we cannot name them all. Rhubarb leaves, for example, either raw or cooked, can cause death or violent convulsions. Peach, elderberry,

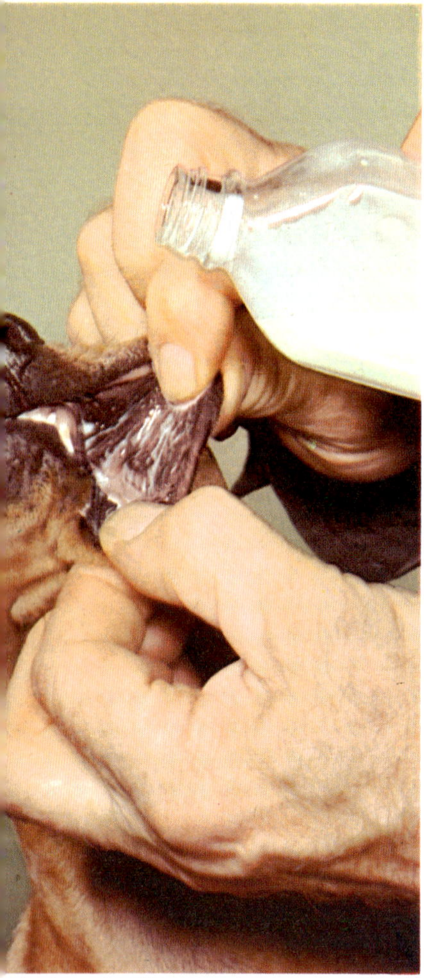

Whenever you have to administer liquid medicine, the proper way to do it is to grasp the dog's lips and form a pocket, into which you can carefully pour the liquid. Never pour directly down the dog's throat. Photo, Sally Anne Thompson.

and cherry trees can cause cyanide poisoning if their bark is consumed.

There are also many insects poisonous to dogs such as cockroaches, spiders, flies, and butterflies. Toads and frogs exude a fluid that can make a dog foam at the mouth—and even kill him—if he bites too hard!

There have been cases of dogs suffering nicotine poisoning by consuming the contents of full ashtrays which thoughtless smokers have left on the coffee table. Also, do not leave nails, staples, pins, or other sharp objects lying around and don't let your puppy play with plastic bags which could suffocate him. Unplug, remove, or cover any electrical cords or wires near your dog. Chewing live wires could lead to severe mouth burns or death. Remember that an ounce of prevention is worth a pound of cure: keep all potentially dangerous objects out of your pet's reach.

PROTECT YOURSELF FIRST

In almost all first aid situations, the dog is in pain. He may also be in shock and not appear to be suffering, that is until you move him. Then he may bite your hand or resist being helped at all. So if you want to help your dog, help yourself first by tying his mouth closed. To do this, use a piece of strong cloth four inches wide and three feet long, depending on the size of the dog. Make a loop in the middle of the strip and slip it over his nose with the knot under his chin and over the bony part of his nose. Pull it tight and bring the ends back around his head behind the ears and tie it tightly, ending with a bow knot for quick, easy release. Now you can handle the dog safely. As a dog perspires through his tongue, do not leave the "emergency muzzle" on any longer than necessary.

ADMINISTERING MEDICINE

When you are giving liquid medicine to your dog, it is a good idea to pull the lips away from the side of the mouth, form a lip pocket, and let the liquid trickle past the tongue. Remain at his side, never in front of the dog, as he may cough and spray you with the liquid. Moreover, you must never pour liquid medicine directly on the tongue as inhalation pneumonia could be the disastrous result.

In some breeds, periodically the anal glands have to be expressed. These glands are located on either side of the dog's anus, and it is a procedure that is best left to a veterinarian.

Medicine in pill form is best administered by forcing the dog's mouth open, holding his head back, and placing the capsule as far back on his tongue as you can reach. Put the palm of your hand over the dog's muzzle (his foreface) with your fingers on one side of his jaw, your thumb on the other. Press his lips hard against his teeth while using your other hand to pull down his lower jaw. With your two fingers, try to put the pill as far back on the dog's tongue as you can reach. Keep his mouth and nostrils closed and he should be forced to swallow the medicine. As the dog will not be feeling well, stroke his neck to comfort him and to help him swallow his medicine more easily. Do keep an eye on him for a few moments afterward, however, to make certain that he does not spit it out.

Pilling a dog is not difficult to do; just ask the veterinarian to show you how it is done. Simply press the dog's lips against his teeth until he opens his mouth (bottom). Then place the pill as far back on the tongue as you can get it (facing page). Now hold the dog's mouth closed and wait to see that he has swallowed. Praise him for being so cooperative. Photo, Sally Anne Thompson.

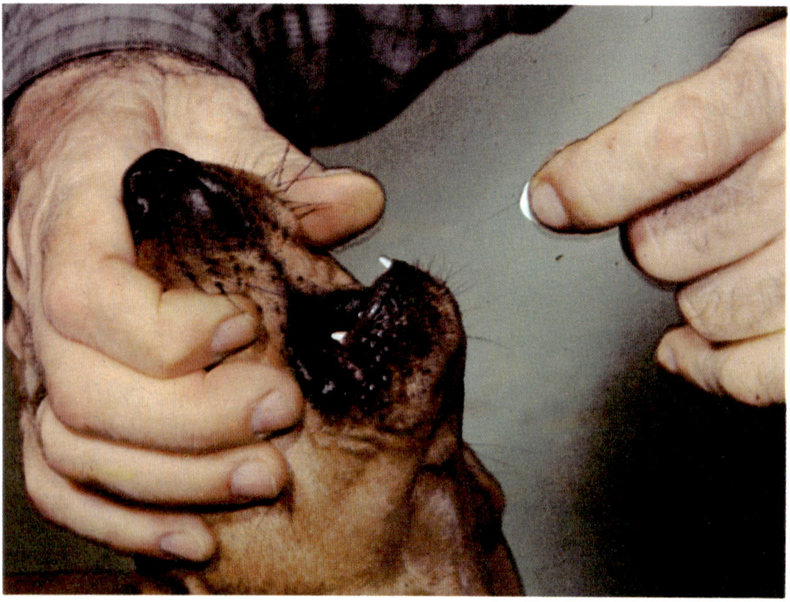

IN CASE OF AN ACCIDENT

It is often difficult for you to assess the dog's injuries after a road accident. He may appear normal but there might be internal hemorrhaging. A vital organ could be damaged or ribs broken. Keep the dog as quiet and warm as possible; cover him with blankets or your coat to let his own body heat build up. Signs of shock are a rapid and weak pulse, glassy-eyed appearance, subnormal temperature, and slow capillary refill time. To determine the last symptom, press firmly against the dog's gums until they turn white. Release and count the number of seconds until the gums return to their normal color. If it is more than 2-3 seconds, the dog may be going into shock. Failure to return to the reddish pink color indicates the dog may be in serious trouble and needs immediate assistance.

If artificial respiration is required, first open the dog's mouth and check for obstructions; extend his tongue and examine the pharynx. Clear his mouth of mucus and blood and hold the mouth slightly open. Mouth-to-mouth resuscitation involves holding the dog's tongue to the bottom of his

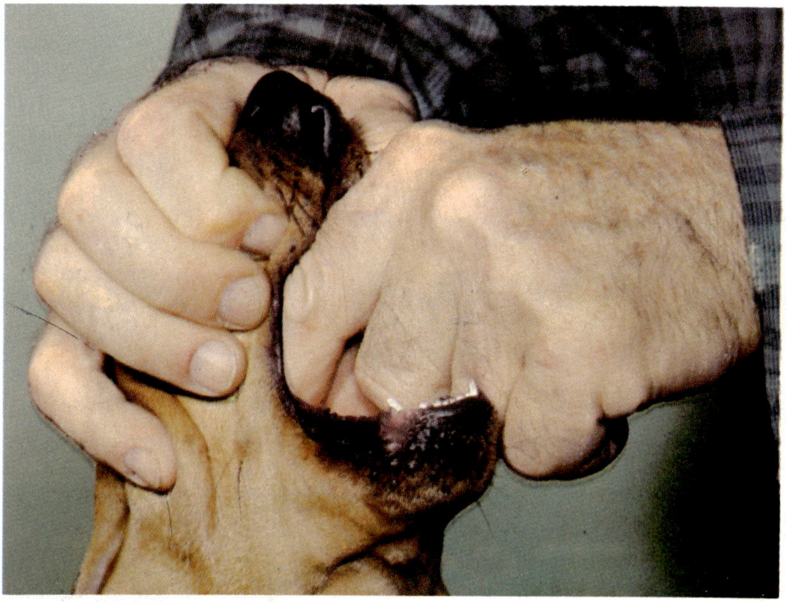

mouth with one hand and sealing his nostrils with the other while you blow into his mouth. Watch for his chest to rise with each inflation. Repeat every 5-6 seconds or 10-12 breaths a minute.

If the veterinarian cannot come to you try to improvise a stretcher to take the dog to him. To carry a puppy, wrap him in a blanket that has been folded into several thicknesses. If he is in shock, it is better to pick him up by holding one hand under his chest, the other under the hindquarters. This will keep him stretched out.

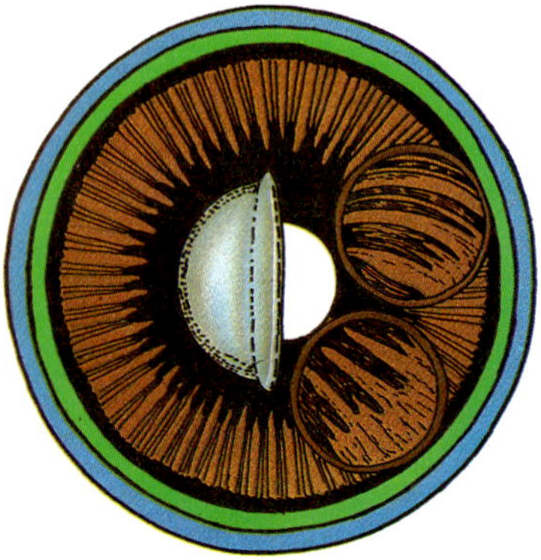

Posterior view of a dog's eye with the lens sectioned.

It is always better to roll an injured dog than to try and lift him. Suppose you find him lying beside the road after a car accident. Apply a muzzle even if you have to use someone's necktie to make one. Send someone for a blanket and roll him gently onto it. Two people, one on each side, can make a stretcher out of the blanket and move the dog easily.

If no blanket is available and the injured dog must be moved, try to keep him as flat as possible. So many dogs' backs are broken in car accidents that one must first consider that possibility. However, if he can move his hind legs or tail, his spine is probably not broken. Get medical assistance for him immediately.

It should be mentioned that unfortunate car accidents, which can maim or kill your dog, can be avoided if he is confined at all times either indoors or, if out-of-doors, in a fenced-in yard or some other protective enclosure. *Never* allow your dog to roam free; even a well-trained dog may, for some unknown reason, dart into the street—and the result could be tragic.

If you need to walk your dog, leash him first so that he will be protected from moving vehicles.

PROTECTING YOUR PET

It is important to watch for any tell-tale signs of illness so that you can spare your pet any unnecessary suffering. Your dog's eyes, for example, should normally be bright and alert, so if the haw is bloodshot or partially covers the eye, it may be a sign of illness or irritation. If your dog has matter in the corners of his eyes, bathe them with a mild eye wash; obtain ointment or eye drops from your veterinarian to treat a chronic condition.

If your dog seems to have something wrong with his ears which causes him to scratch at them or shake his head, cautiously probe the ear with a cotton swab. An accumulation of wax will probably work itself out. Dirt or dried blood, however, is indicative of ear mites or infection and should be treated immediately. Sore ears in the summer, due to insect bites, should be washed with mild soap and water, then covered with a soothing ointment and wrapped in gauze if necessary. Keep your pet away from insects until his ears heal, even if this means confining him indoors.

INOCULATIONS

Periodic check-ups by your veterinarian throughout your puppy's life is good health insurance. The person from whom your puppy was purchased should tell you what inoculations your puppy has had and when the next visit to the vet is necessary. You must make certain that your puppy has been vaccinated against the following infectious canine diseases: distemper, canine hepatitis, leptospirosis, rabies, parvovirus, and parainfluenza. Annual "boosters" thereafter provide inexpensive protection for your dog against such serious diseases. Puppies should also be checked for worms at an early age.

DISTEMPER

Young dogs are most susceptible to distemper, although it may affect dogs of all ages. Signs of the disease are loss of appetite, depression, chills, and fever, as well as a watery discharge from the eyes and nose. Unless treated promptly, the disease goes into advanced stages with infections of the lungs, intestines, and nervous system. Dogs that recover may be impaired with

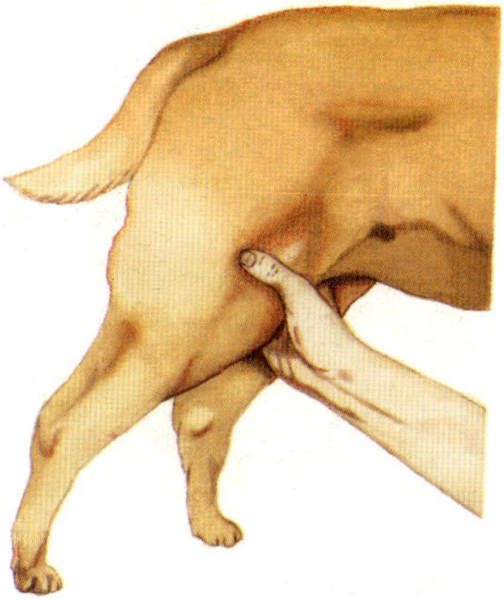

You can find your dog's femoral artery on the inner surface of one of the hind legs. Press gently but firmly and soon you will find the pulse.

paralysis, convulsions, a twitch, or some other defect, usually spastic in nature. Early inoculations in puppyhood should be followed by an annual booster to help protect against this disease.

CANINE HEPATITIS

The initial symptoms of hepatitis are drowsiness, vomiting, loss of appetite, high temperature, and great thirst. Often these symptoms are accompanied by swellings of the head, neck, and abdomen. This disease strikes quickly, and death may occur in only a few hours. An annual booster shot is needed after the initial series of puppy shots.

LEPTOSPIROSIS

Infection is begun by the dog's

An Elizabethan collar can be fashioned from corrugated cardboard. When slipped over a dog's neck, it keeps him from getting at a wound or suture.

Skeletal deformities are largely related to poor diet during the early years of a dog's life. This is one reason why good nutrition is important.

licking substances contaminated by the urine or feces of infected animals, and the disease is carried by bacteria that live in stagnant or slow-moving water. The symptoms are diarrhea and a yellowish-brownish discoloration of the jaws, teeth, and tongue, caused by an inflammation of the kidneys. A veterinarian can administer the leptospirosis shot along with the distemper and hepatitis shot.

RABIES

This disease of the dog's central nervous system spreads by infectious saliva which is transmitted by the bite of an infected animal. Of the two main classes of symptoms, the first is "furious rabies," in which the dog shows a period of melancholy or depression, then irritation, and finally paralysis. The first period can be from a few hours to several days, and during this time the dog is cross and will change his position often, lose his appetite, begin to lick, and bite or swallow foreign objects. During this phase the dog is spasmodically wild and has impulses to run away. The dog acts fearless and bites everything in sight. If he is caged or confined, he will fight at the bars and possibly break teeth or fracture his jaw. His bark becomes a peculiar howl. In the final stage, the animal's lower jaw becomes paralyzed and hangs down. He then walks with a stagger, and saliva drips from his mouth. About four to eight days after the onset of paralysis, the dog dies.

The second class of symptoms is referred to as "dumb rabies" and is characterized by the dog's walking in a bearlike manner with his head down. The lower jaw is paralyzed and the dog is unable to bite. It appears as if he has a bone caught in his throat.

If a dog is bitten by a rabid animal, he probably can be saved if he is taken to a veterinarian in time for a series of injections. After the symptoms appear, however, no cure is possible. The local health department must be notified in the case of a rabid dog, for this is a danger to all who come near him. As with the other shots each year, an annual rabies inoculation is very important. In many areas, the administration of rabies vaccines for dogs is required by law.

PARVOVIRUS

This relatively new virus is a contagious disease that has spread in almost epidemic proportions throughout certain sections of the United States. Also, it has appeared in Australia, Canada, and Europe. Canine parvovirus attacks the intestinal tract, white blood cells, and heart muscle. It is believed to spread through dog-to-dog contact, and the specific course of infection seems to come from fecal matter of infected dogs. Overcoming parvovirus is difficult, for it is capable of existing in the environment for many months under varying conditions and temperatures, and it can be transmitted from place to place on the hair and feet of infected dogs, as well as on the clothes and shoes of people.

Vomiting and severe diarrhea, which will appear within five to seven days after the animal has been exposed to the virus, are the initial signs of this disease. At the onset of illness, feces will be light gray or yellow-gray in color, and the urine might be blood-streaked. Because of the vomiting and severe diarrhea, the dog that has contracted the disease will dehydrate quickly. Depression and loss of appetite, as well as a rise in temperature, can accompany the other symptoms. Death caused by this disease usually occurs within 48 to 72 hours following the appearance of the symptoms.

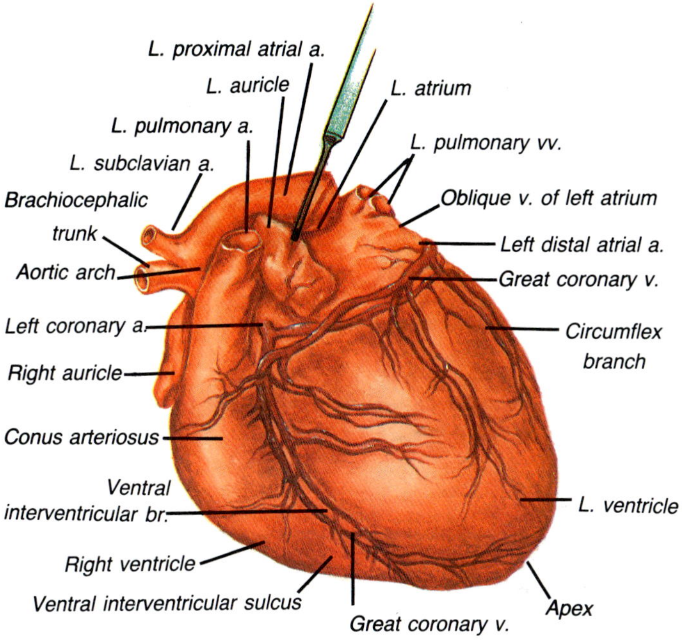

Left lateral view of the canine heart.

Puppies are hardest hit, and the virus is fatal to 75 percent of puppies that contract it. Death in puppies can be within two days of the onset of the illness.

A series of shots administered by a veterinarian is the best preventive measure for canine parvovirus. It is also important to disinfect the area where the dog is housed by using one part sodium hypochlorite solution (household bleach) to thirty parts of water and to keep the dog from coming into contact with the fecal matter of other dogs.

PARAINFLUENZA

Parainfluenza, or infectious canine tracheobronchitis, is commonly known as "kennel cough." It is highly contagious, affects the upper respiratory system, and is spread through direct or indirect contact with already diseased dogs. It will readily infect dogs of all ages that have not been vaccinated or that were previously infected. While this condition is definitely one of the serious diseases in dogs, it is self-limiting, usually

Dorsal view of the canine heart.

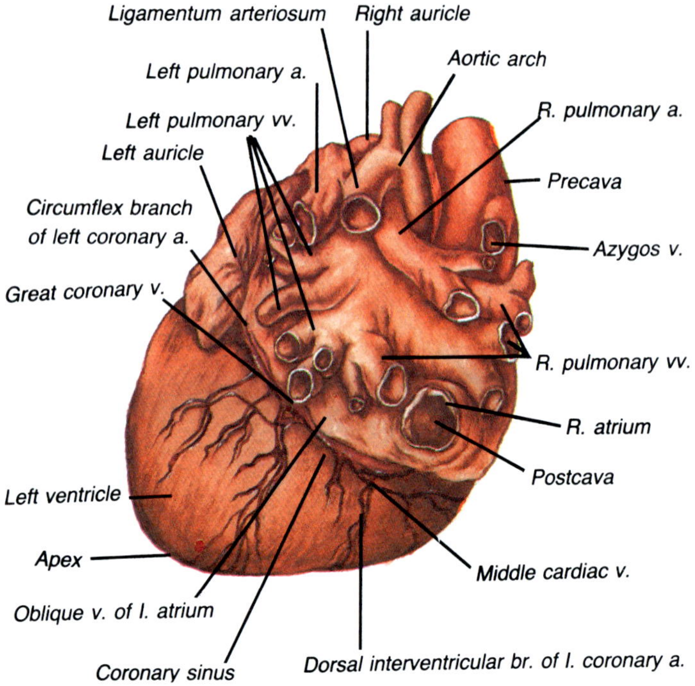

lasting only two to four weeks. The symptoms are high fever and intense, harsh coughing that brings up mucus. As long as your pet sees your veterinarian immediately, the chances for his complete recovery are excellent.

EXTERNAL PARASITES

A parasite is an animal that lives in or on an organism of another species known as the host. The majority of dogs' skin problems are parasitic in nature and an estimated 90% of puppies are born with parasites.

Ticks can cause serious problems to dogs where the latter have access to woods, fields, and vegetation in which large numbers of native mammals live. Ticks are usually found clinging to vegetation and attach themselves to animals passing by. They have eight legs and a heavy shield or shell-like covering on their upper surface. Only by keeping dogs away from tick-infested areas can ticks on dogs be prevented.

The flea is the single most common cause of skin and coat problems in dogs. There are 11,000 kinds of fleas which can transmit specific disorders like tapeworm and heartworm or transport smaller parasites onto your dog. The common tapeworm, for example, requires the flea as an intermediate host for completion of its life cycle. A female flea can lay hundreds of eggs and these will become adults in less than three weeks. Depending on the temperature and the amount of moisture, large numbers of fleas can attack dogs, and the ears of dogs, in particular, can play host to hundreds of fleas.

Fleas can lurk in crevices and cracks, carpets, and bedding for months, so frequent cleaning of your dog's environment is absolutely essential. If he is infected by other dogs, then have him bathed and "dipped," which means that he will be put into water containing a chemical that kills fleas. Your veterinarian will advise which dip to use and your dog must be bathed for at least twenty minutes. These parasites are tenacious and remarkably agile creatures; fleas have existed since prehistoric times and have been found in arctic as well as tropical climates. Some experts claim that fleas can jump 150 times the length of their bodies; this makes them difficult to catch and kill. Thus, treating your pet for parasites without simultaneously treating the environment is both inefficient and ineffective.

A dog's knee joint is referred to as the stifle, and it is formed by the articulation of the upper and lower thighs.

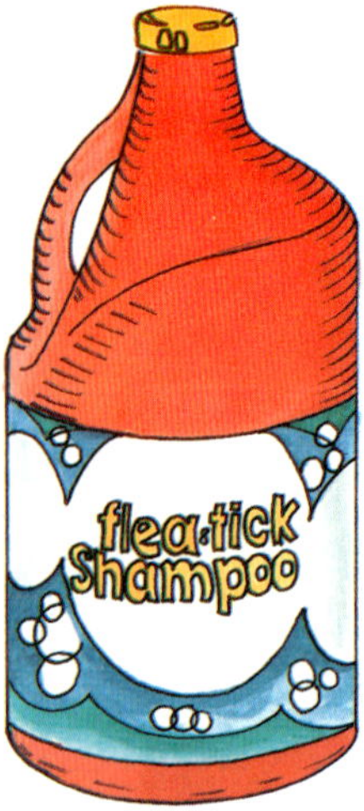

During the warm weather, you may have to bathe your dog with a flea and tick shampoo to keep these pesky parasites under control.

INTERNAL PARASITES

Four common internal parasites that may infect a dog are: roundworms, hookworms, whipworms, and tapeworms. The first three can be diagnosed by laboratory examination of the dog's stool, and tapeworms can be determined by seeing segments in the stool or attached to the hair around the anus. When a veterinarian determines what type of worm or worms are present, he then can advise the best treatment.

Roundworms, the dog's most common intestinal parasite, have a life cycle which permits complete eradication by worming twice, ten days apart. The first worming will remove all adults and the second will destroy all subsequently hatched eggs before they, in turn, can produce more parasites.

A dog in good physical condition is less susceptible to worm infestation than a weak dog. Proper sanitation and a nutritious diet help in preventing worms. One of the best preventive measures is to have clean, dry bedding for the dog, as this diminishes the possibility of reinfection due to flea or tick bites.

Heartworm infestation in dogs is passed by mosquitoes. Dogs with this disease tire easily, have difficulty in breathing, and lose

There are many shampoos on the market, each one meant for a different purpose. This protein shampoo is a good all-purpose shampoo.

weight despite a hearty appetite. Administration of preventive medicine throughout the spring, summer, and fall months is advised. A veterinarian must first take a blood sample from the dog to test for the presence of the disease, and if the dog is heartworm-free, pills or liquid medicine can be prescribed to protect against any infestation.

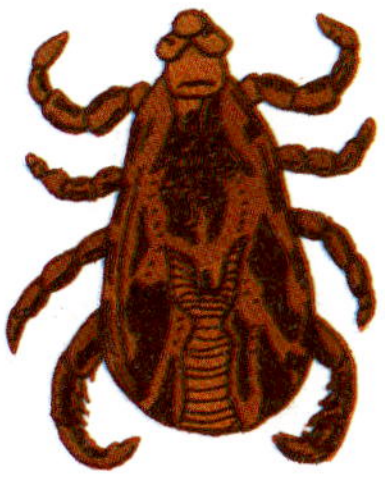

If you spend a great deal of time outdoors with your dog, it is important to check his coat for ticks.

CANINE SENIOR CITIZENS

The processes of aging and gradual degenerative changes start far earlier in a dog than often observed, usually at about seven years of age. If we recall that each year of a dog's life roughly corresponds to about seven years in the life of a man, by the age of seven he is well into middle age. Your pet will become less active, will have a poorer appetite with increased thirst, there will be frequent periods of constipation and less than normal passage of urine.

Red mange, a skin disorder, is caused by the mite Demodex folliculorum.

His skin and coat might become dull and dry and his hair will become thin and fall out. There is a tendency towards obesity in old age, which should be avoided by maintaining a regular exercise program. Remember, also, that your pet will be less able to cope with extreme heat, cold, fatigue, and change in routine.

There is the possibility of loss or impairment of hearing or eyesight. He may become bad-tempered more often than in the past. Other ailments such as rheumatism, arthritis, kidney infections, heart disease, male prostatism, and hip dysplasia may occur. Of course, all these require a veterinarian's examination and recommendation of suitable treatment. Care of the teeth is also important in the aging dog. Indeed, the mouth can be a barometer of nutritional health. Degenerating gums, heavy tartar on the teeth, loose teeth, and sore lips are common. The worst of all diseases in old age, however, is neglect. Good care in early life will have its effect on your dog's later years; the nutrition and general health care of his first few years can determine his lifespan and the quality of his life. It is worth bearing in mind that the older, compared to the younger, animal needs more protein of good biological value, more vitamins A, B-complex, D and E, more calcium and iron, less fat and fewer carbohydrates.

The companionship of pets, not only to children and adults, but particularly to the aged and lonely, cannot be overestimated. Therefore, a dog's grateful owner should do all he can to enhance and prolong the life of his cherished companion. Regular doses of TLC or Tender Loving Care is the best "medicine" your dog can receive throughout his life.

DEATH OF A FRIEND

What can you do, however, for a pet who is so sick or severely injured that he will never recover his normal health? Although one is often extremely reluctant to consider the suggestion, sometimes the kindest and most humane solution is to have your veterinarian put him out of his misery by inducing his death peacefully and painlessly. This process is called euthanasia, a word of Greek derivation meaning "easy or good death." It is usually carried out by having your veterinarian inject a death-inducing drug or an overdose of anesthetic.

Such a decision will probably be an extremely difficult one for you to make but you need not, in fact, should not, make it alone. Your veterinarian should be your chief adviser and family and friends can assist in the decision-making process. Your children should not be excluded from this painful time; it would be inadvisable to attempt to "shield" or "protect" them from such events which are an inevitable part of life. They would suffer even more if, later, they did not understand how or why their beloved pet had died.

By remembering the wonderful times with your pet, by talking about him to family and friends, by remembering him as healthy and full of life, you will eventually cope with your grief. It is perfectly natural to grieve for the loss of such a loyal, affectionate companion who has provided you with so many happy memories. People who do not have pets often fail to realize what a very important part of our lives these animals fill and what a void is created by their absence. Others are more sympathetic and compassionate. Rest assured, however, that if you have chosen a painless, eternal sleep for your pet by "putting him to sleep" (an appropriate euphemism in this case), you have done him a final service as a loving, considerate friend.

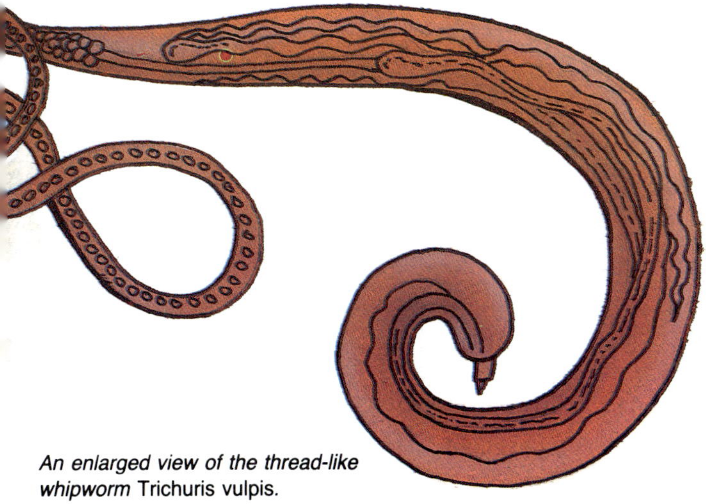

An enlarged view of the thread-like whipworm Trichuris vulpis.

If you own a bitch and you want to breed her, first make sure you can handle the responsibility of caring for her and her litter of pups. Consider the time and money involved just to get her into breeding condition and then to sustain her throughout

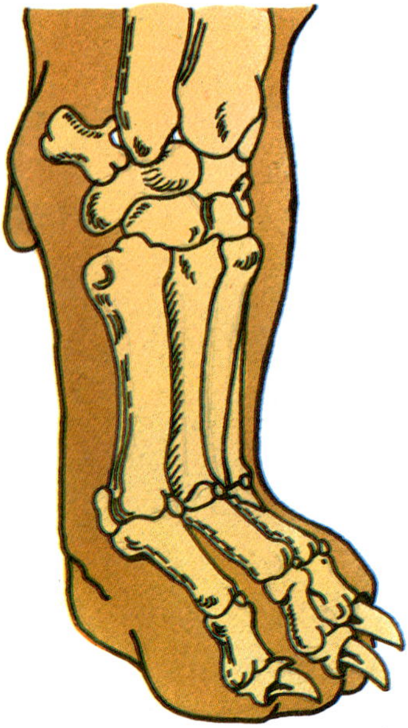

If your dog is not exposed to rough surfaces, such as asphalt, then his nails will have to be clipped periodically.

pregnancy and afterwards while she tends her young. You will be obligated to house, feed, groom, and housebreak the puppies until good homes can be found for them; and, lest we forget, there will be periodic trips to the vet for check-ups, wormings, and inoculations. Common sense should tell you that it is indeed cruel to bring unwanted or unplanned puppies into an already crowded canine world; only negligent pet owners allow this to happen. With pet-quality purebred dogs, most breeders require prospective pet owners to sign a neuter/spay agreement when they purchase their dogs. In this way breeders can be assured that only their very best stock of show-quality and breeder-quality animals, i.e., those that match closely their individual standards of perfection and those that are free of genetic disorders or disease, will be used to propagate the breed.

Before you select a stud to mate with your bitch, think carefully about why you want her to give birth to a litter of puppies. If you feel she will be deprived in some way if she is not bred, if you think your children will learn from the experience, if you have the mistaken notion that you will make money from this great undertaking, think again. A dog can lead a perfectly happy, healthy, normal life without having been mated; in fact, spaying a female and neutering a male helps them become better pets, as they are not so anxious to search for a mate in an effort to relieve their sexual tensions. As for giving the children a lesson in sex education, this is hardly a valid reason for breeding your dog. And on an economic level, it takes not only years of hard work (researching pedigrees and bloodlines, studying genetics, among other things), but it takes plenty of capital (money, equipment, facilities) to make a decent profit from dog breeding. Why most dedicated breeders are lucky just to break even. If you have only a casual interest in dog breeding, it is best to leave this pastime to those who are more experienced in such matters, those who consider it a serious hobby or vocation. If you have bought a breeder– or show-quality canine, one that may be capable of producing champions, and if you are just starting out with this breeding venture, seek advice from the seller of your dog, from other veteran breeders, and from your veterinarian before you begin.

THE FEMALE "IN SEASON"

A bitch may come into season (also known as "heat" or estrus) once or several times a year, depending on the particular breed and the individual dog. Her first seasonal period, that is to say, the time when she is capable of being fertilized by a male dog, may occur as early as six months with some breeds. If you own a female and your intention is *not* to breed her, by all means discuss with the vet the possibility of having her spayed: this means before she reaches sexual maturity.

Anti-mating spray is useful when a bitch is in heat. By spraying this product around and near the bitch, you will keep would-be canine suitors away.

The first sign of the female's being in season is a thin red discharge, which may increase for about a week; it then changes

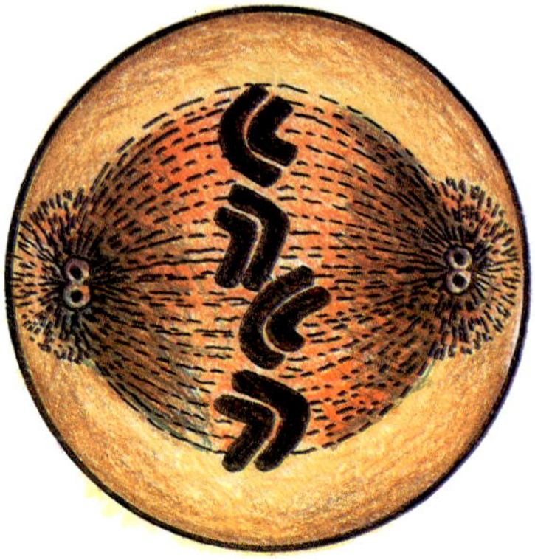

Cell division is known as mitosis. In the top left photo, the chromosomes become thicker and more obvious in the nucleus of the cell. A web of fibers (the spindle) forms and covers the middle of the cell in the top right photo. The nucleus has disappeared and the chromosomes have split and are being pulled to opposite sides of the cell. Below, the cell becomes two and mitosis is complete.

color to a thin yellowish stain, which lasts about another week. Simultaneously, there is a swelling of the vulva, the exterior portion of the female's reproductive tract; the soft, flabby vulva indicates her readiness to mate. Around this second week or so ovulation occurs, and this is the crucial period for her to be bred, if this is what you have in mind for her. It is during this middle phase of the heat cycle when conception can take place. Just remember that there is great variation from bitch to bitch with regard to how often they come into heat, how long the heat cycles last, how long the period of ovulation lasts, and how much time elapses between heat cycles. Generally, after the third week of heat, the vulval swelling decreases and the estrus period ceases for several months.

It should be mentioned that the female will probably lose her puppy coat, or at least shed part of it, about three months after she has come into season. This is the time when her puppies

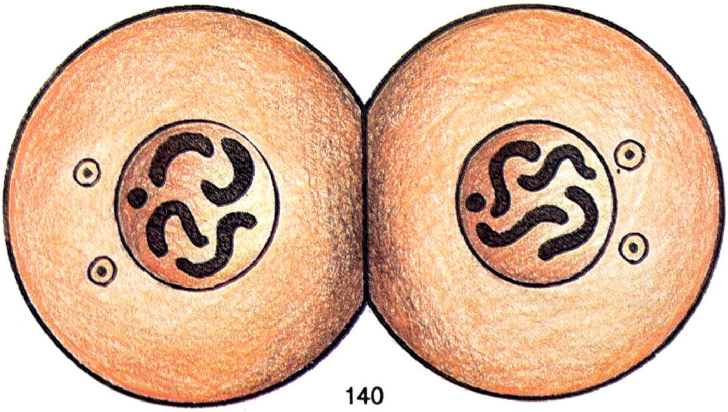

would have been weaned, had she been mated, and females generally drop coat at this time.

With female dogs, there are few, if any, behavioral changes during estrus. A bitch may dart out of an open door to greet all available male dogs that show an interest in her, and she may occasionally raise her tail and assume a mating stance, particularly if you pet her lower back; but these signs are not as dramatic as those of the sexually mature male. He himself does not experience heat cycles; rather, he is attracted to the female during all phases of her seasonal period. He usually becomes more aggressive and tends to fight with other males, especially over females in heat. He tends to mark his territory with urine to attract females and at the same time to warn other competitive males. It is not uncommon to see him mount various objects, and people, in an effort to satisfy his mature sexual urges.

If you are a homeowner and you have an absolutely climb-proof and dig-proof run within your yard, it may be safe to leave your bitch in season there. But then again it may not be a wise idea, as there have been cases of males mating with females right through chain-link fencing! Just to be on the safe side, shut her indoors during her heat periods and don't let her outdoors until you are certain the estrus period is over. Never leave a bitch in heat outdoors, unsupervised, even for a minute so that she can defecate or urinate. If you want to prevent the neighborhood dogs from

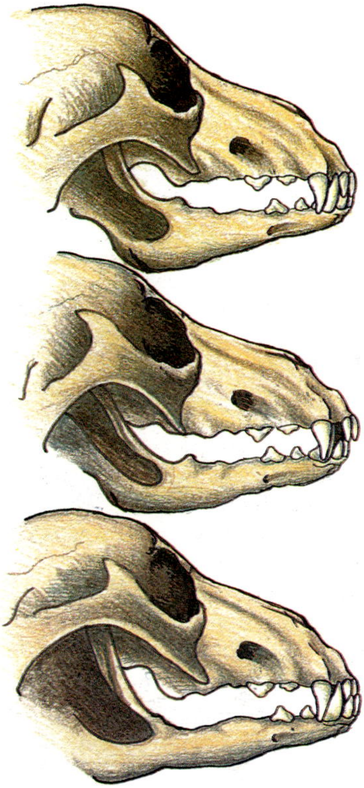

Three types of bites seen in dogs: top, scissors (the most common); middle, overshot; and bottom, undershot (seen in Bulldogs).

hanging around your doorstep, as they inevitably will do when they discover your female is in season, take her some distance away from the house before you let her do her business. Otherwise, these canine suitors will be attracted to her by the arousing odor of her urine, and they will know instinctively that she isn't far from her scented "calling card." If you need to walk your bitch, take her in the car to a nearby park or field for a chance to stretch her legs. Remember that after about three weeks, and this varies from dog to dog, you can let her outdoors again with no worry that she can have puppies until the next heat period.

WHEN TO BREED

It is usually best to breed a bitch when she comes into her second or third season. Plan in advance the time of year which is best for you, taking into account your own schedule of activities (vacations, business trips, social

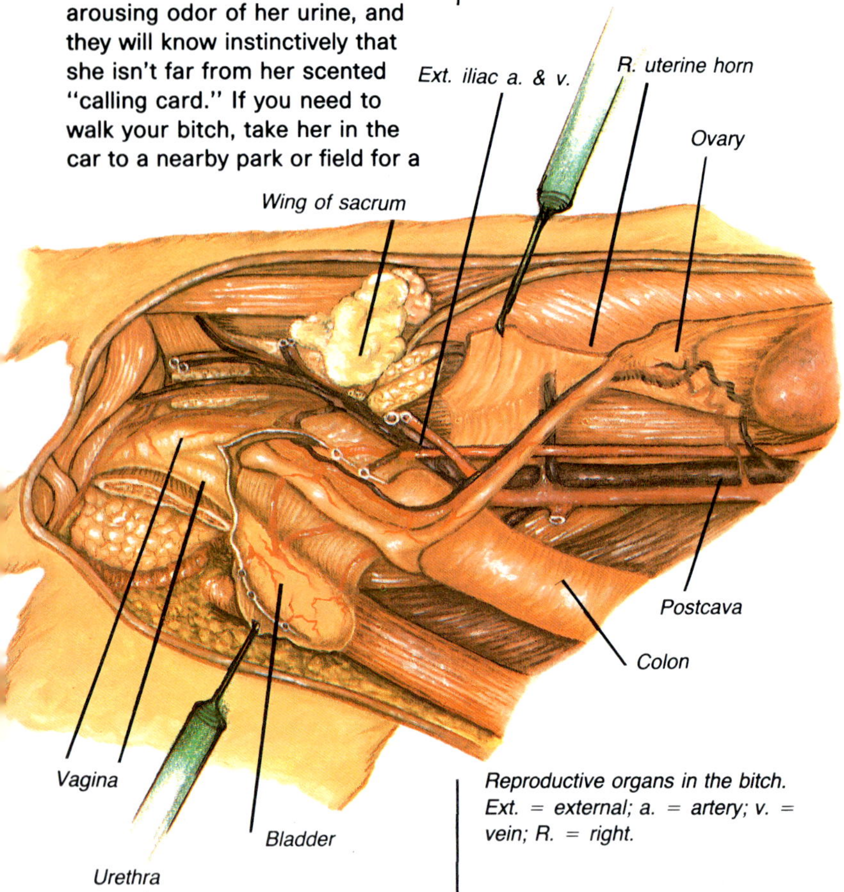

Reproductive organs in the bitch. Ext. = external; a. = artery; v. = vein; R. = right.

engagements, and so on). Make sure you will be able to set aside plenty of time to assist with whelping of the newborn pups and caring for the dam and her litter for the next few weeks. At the very least, it probably will take an hour or so each day just to feed and clean up after the brood—but undoubtedly you will find it takes much longer if you stop to admire and play with the youngsters periodically! Refrain from selling the litter until it is at least six weeks old, keeping in mind that a litter of pups takes up a fair amount of space by then. It will be your responsibility to provide for them until they have been weaned from their

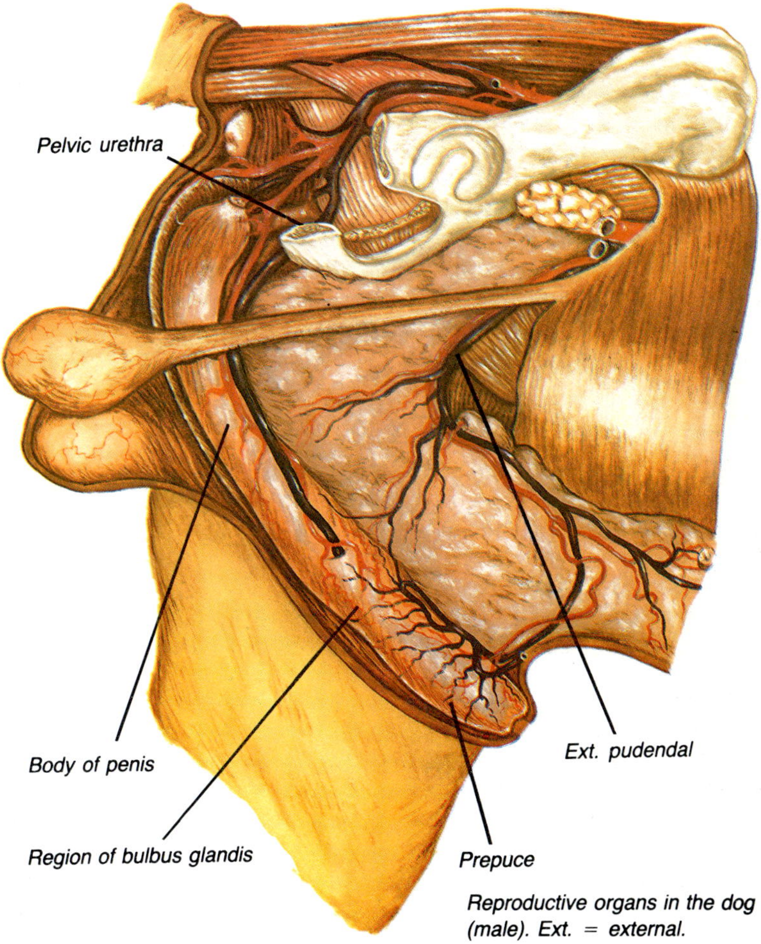

Reproductive organs in the dog (male). Ext. = external.

mother, properly socialized, housebroken, and ready to go to new homes (unless you plan to keep them all). Hopefully, as strongly recommended, you will have already lined up buyers for the pups in advance of their arrival into this world.

CHOOSING THE STUD You can plan to breed your female about six-and-one-half months after the start of her last season, although a variation of a month or two either way is not unusual. Do some research into the various bloodlines within your breed and then choose a stud dog and make arrangements well in advance. If you are breeding for show stock, which will command higher prices than pet-quality animals, a mate should be chosen very carefully. He should complement any deficiencies (bad traits) that your female may have, and he should have a good show record or be the sire of show winners, if he is old enough to have proven himself. If possible, the bitch and stud should have several ancestors in common within the last two or three generations, as such combinations have been known, generally, to "click" best.

The owner of a stud dog usually charges a stud fee for use of the animal's services. This does not always guarantee a litter, but if she fails to conceive, chances are you may be able to breed your female to that stud again. In some instances the owner of the stud will agree to take a "first pick of the litter" in place of a fee. You should, of course, settle all details beforehand, including the possibility of a single puppy surviving, deciding the age at which the pup is to be taken, and so forth.

If you plan to raise a litter that will be sold exclusively as pets, and if you merely plan to make use of an available male (not a top stud dog), the most important selection point involves temperament. Make sure the dog is friendly, as well as healthy, because a bad disposition can be passed on to his puppies—and this is the worst of all traits in a dog destined to be a pet. If you are breeding pet-quality dogs, a "stud fee puppy," not necessarily the choice of the litter, is the usual payment. Don't breed indiscriminately; be sure you will be able to find good homes for each of the pups, or be sure you have the facilities to keep them yourself, *before* you plan to mate your dog.

PREPARATION FOR BREEDING Before you breed your female, make sure she is in good health. She should be neither too thin nor too fat. Any skin disease *must* be cured first so that it is not passed on to the puppies. If she has worms, she should be wormed before being bred or within three weeks after the mating. It is generally considered a good idea to revaccinate her against distemper and hepatitis before the puppies are born. This will increase the immunity the puppies receive during their early, most vulnerable period.

The female will probably be ready to breed twelve days after the first colored discharge appears. You can usually make arrangements to board her with the owner of the stud for a few days, to insure her being there at the proper time; or you can take her to be mated and bring her home the same day if you live near enough to the stud's owner. If the bitch still appears receptive she may be bred again two days later, just to make certain the mating was successful. However, some females never show signs of willingness, so it helps to have an experienced breeder on hand. In fact, you both may have to assist with the mating by holding the animals against each other to ensure the "tie" is not broken, that is, to make certain copulation takes place. Sometimes, too, you'll need to muzzle the bitch to keep her from biting you or the stud.

Usually the second day after the discharge changes color is the proper time to mate the bitch, and she may be bred for about three days following this time. For an additional week or so, she may have some discharge and attract other dogs by her odor; but she should not be bred. Once she has been bred, keep her far from all other male dogs, as they have the capacity to impregnate her again and sire some of her puppies. This could prove disastrous where purebred puppies—especially show-quality ones—are concerned.

Puppies can be transported to the vet in carriers like this one.

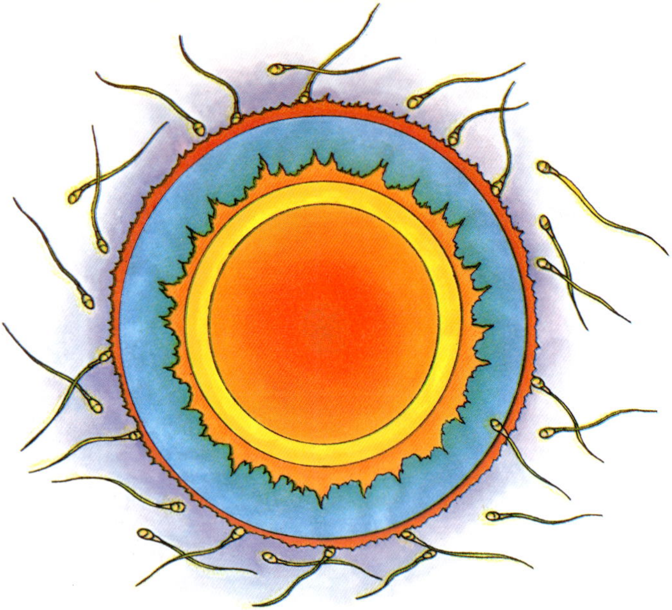

Fertilization of the egg occurs when one sperm penetrates the ovum membrane.

THE FEMALE IN WHELP

You can expect the puppies nine weeks from the day of the mating, although sixty-one days is as common as sixty-three. Gestation, that period when the pups are developing inside their mother, varies among individual bitches. During this time the female should receive normal care and exercise. If she was overweight at the start, don't increase her food right away; excess weight at whelping time can be a problem with some dogs. If she is on the thin side, however, supplement her meal or meals with a portion of milk and biscuit at noontime. This will help build her up and put weight on her.

You may want to add a mineral and vitamin supplement to her diet, on the advice of your veterinarian, since she will need an extra supply not only for herself but for the puppies growing inside of her. As the mother's appetite increases, feed her more. During the last two weeks of pregnancy, the pups grow enormously and the mother will have little room for food and less of an appetite. She should be tempted with meat, liver, and milk, however.

As the female in whelp grows

Facing page: It is important to rid a dog of fleas since these external parasites are intermediate hosts of the tapeworm.

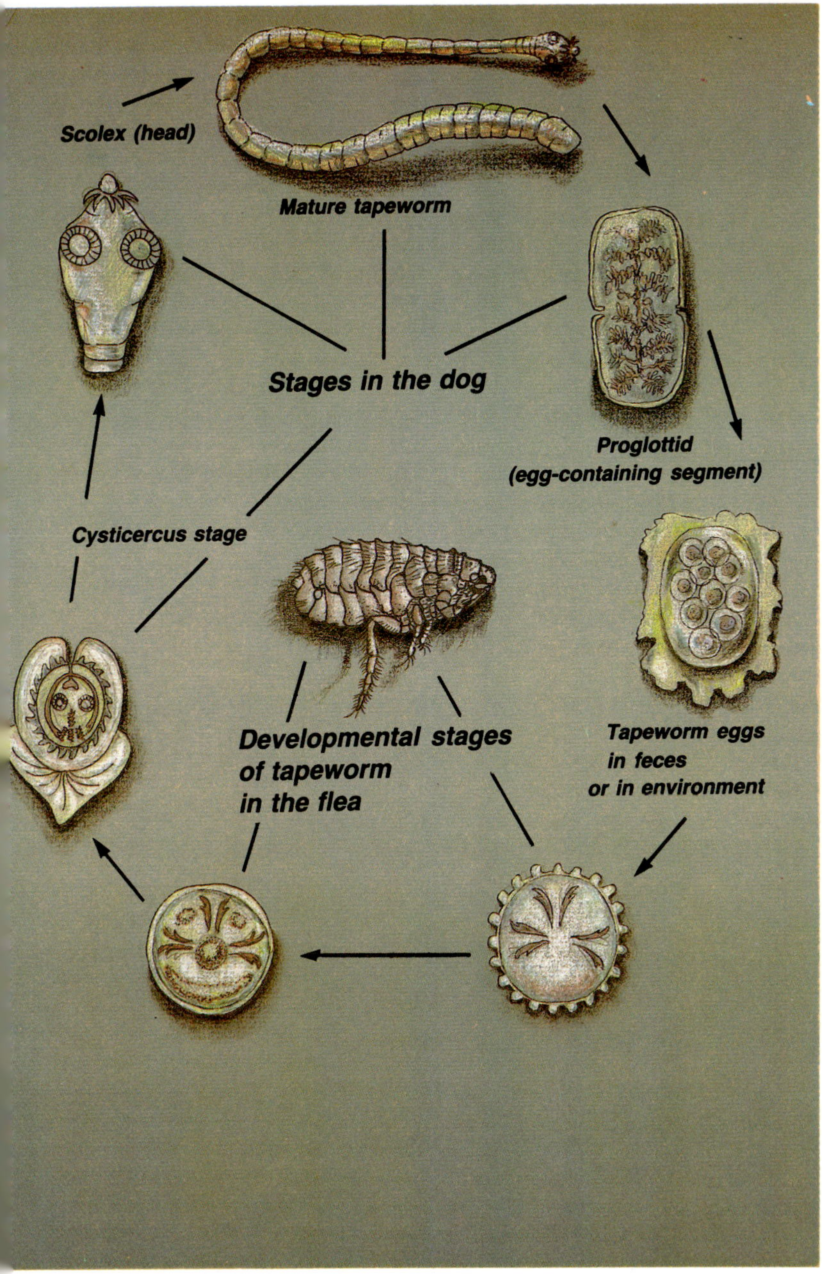
Scolex (head)
Mature tapeworm
Stages in the dog
Proglottid
(egg-containing segment)
Cysticercus stage
Tapeworm eggs
in feces
or in environment
Developmental stages
of tapeworm
in the flea

heavier, cut out violent exercise and jumping from her usual routine. Although a dog used to such activities will often play with the children or run around voluntarily, restrain her for her own sake.

A sign that whelping is imminent is the loss of hair around her breasts. This is nature's way of "clearing a path" so that the puppies will be able to find their source of nourishment. As parturition draws near, the breasts will have swelled with milk and the nipples will have enlarged and darkened to a rosy pink. If the hair in the breast region does not shed for some reason, you can easily cut it short with a pair of scissors or comb it out so that it does not mat and become a hindrance to the suckling pups later on.

PREPARING FOR THE PUPPIES

Prepare a whelping box a few days before the puppies are due, and allow the mother to sleep there overnight or to spend some time in it during the day to become accustomed to it. Then she is less likely to try to have her pups under the front porch or in the middle of your bed. A variety of places will serve, such as a corner of your cellar or garage (provided these places are warm and dry). An unused room, such as a dimly lit spare bedroom, can also serve as the place for delivery. If the weather is warm, a large outdoor dog house will do, as long as it is well protected from rain, drafts, and the cold—and enclosed by fencing or a run. A whelping box serves to separate mother and puppies from visitors and other distractions. The walls should be high enough to restrain the puppies yet low enough to allow the mother to take a short respite from her brood after she has fed them. Four feet square is minimum size (for most dogs) and six-to-eight-inch high walls will keep the pups in until they begin to climb; then side walls should be built up so that the young ones cannot wander away from their nest. As the puppies grow, they really need more room anyway, so double the space with a very low partition down the middle of the box, and soon you will find them naturally housebreaking themselves. Puppies rarely relieve themselves where they sleep.

Layers of newspapers spread over the whole area will make excellent bedding and be absorbent enough to keep the surface warm and dry. These should be removed daily and replaced with another thick layer. An old quilt or washable blanket makes better footing for the nursing puppies than slippery newspaper during the first week; this is also softer for the mother to lie on.

Be prepared for the actual whelping several days in advance. Usually the mother will tear up papers, refuse food, and become restless. These may be false alarms; the real test is her temperature, which will drop to below 100°F about twelve hours before whelping. Take her temperature with a rectal thermometer, morning and evening, and usher her to her whelping box when her temperature goes down. Keep a close watch on her and make sure she stays safely indoors (or outdoors in a safe enclosure); if she is let outside, unleashed, or allowed to roam freely, she could wander off and start to go into labor. It is possible that she could whelp anywhere and this could be unfortunate if she needs your assistance.

WHELPING

Usually little help is needed from you, but it is wise to stay close to make sure that the mother's lack of experience (if this is her first time) does not cause an unnecessary complication. Be ready to help when the first puppy arrives, for it could smother if she does not break the amniotic membrane enclosing it. She should tear open the sac and start licking the puppy, drying and stimulating it. Check to see that all fluids have been cleared from the pup's nostrils and mouth after the mother has licked her youngster

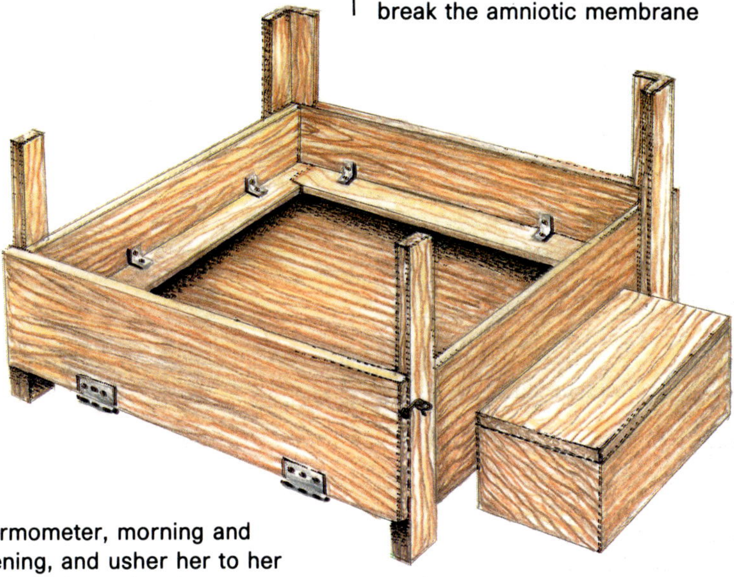

It is a wise idea to supply a pregnant bitch with a whelping box; otherwise she may give birth to her pups in some undesirable place.

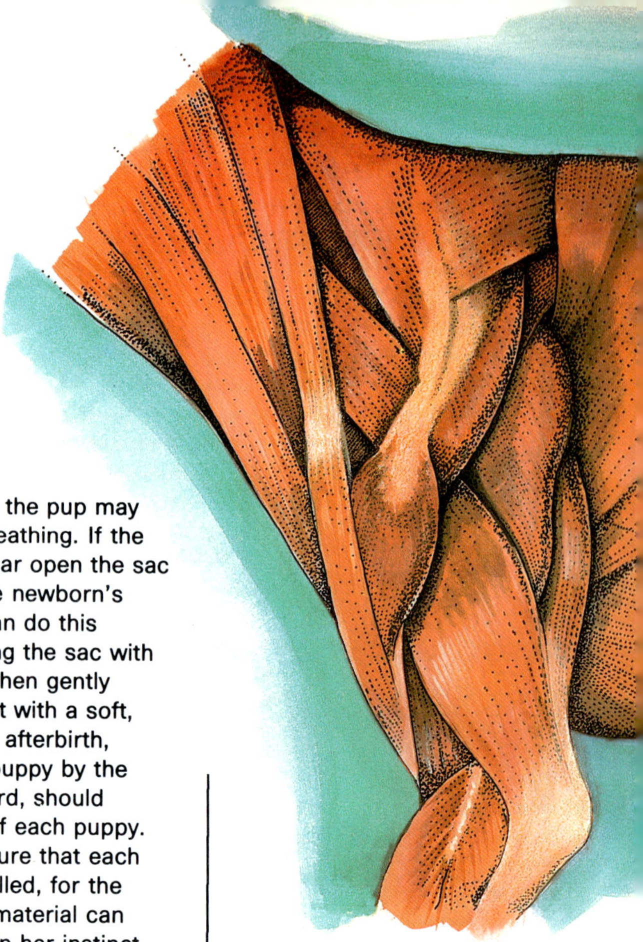

clean; otherwise, the pup may have difficulty breathing. If the mother fails to tear open the sac and stimulate the newborn's breathing, you can do this yourself by tearing the sac with your hands and then gently rubbing the infant with a soft, rough towel. The afterbirth, attached to the puppy by the long umbilical cord, should follow the birth of each puppy. Watch to make sure that each afterbirth is expelled, for the retaining of this material can cause infection. In her instinct for cleanliness the mother will probably eat the afterbirth after severing the umbilical cord. One or two meals of this will not hurt her; they stimulate her milk supply, as well as labor, for remaining pups. But eating too many afterbirths can make her lose appetite for the food she needs to feed her pups and regain her strength. So remove the rest of them, along with the wet newspapers, and keep the box dry and clean.

If the mother does not bite the cord, or bites it too close to the puppy's body, take over the job to prevent an umbilical hernia. Tearing is recommended; but you can cut the cord, about two inches from the body, with a sawing motion of scissors that have been sterilized in alcohol. Then dip the end of the cut cord in a shallow dish of iodine; the cord will dry up and fall off in a few days.

The puppies should follow

Shoulder musculature. Regular exercise is important to keep your dog physically fit—to keep the muscles lean and supple.

each other at intervals of not more than half an hour. If more time goes past and you are sure there are still pups to come, taking the mother for a brisk walk outside may start labor again. If she is actively straining without producing a puppy, the youngster may be presented backward, a so-called "breech" birth. Careful assistance with a well-lubricated finger to feel for the puppy or ease it back may help, but never attempt to pull it out by force. This could cause serious damage, so seek the services of an expert—your veterinarian or an experienced breeder.

If *anything* seems wrong, during labor or parturition, waste no time in calling your veterinarian who can examine the bitch and, if necessary, give her hormones to stimulate the birth of the remaining puppies. You may want his experience in whelping the litter even if all goes well. He will probably prefer to have the puppies born at his hospital rather than to get up in the middle of the night to come to your home. The mother would, no doubt, prefer to stay at home; but you can be sure she will get the best of care in a veterinary hospital. If the puppies are born at home and all goes as it should, watch the mother carefully afterward. Within a day or two of the birth, it is wise to have the veterinarian check her and the pups to ensure all is well.

Make sure each puppy finds a teat and starts nursing right away, as these first few meals supply colostral antibodies to help the pup fight disease. As soon as he is dry, hold each puppy to a nipple for a good meal without competition. Then he may join his littermates in the whelping box, out of his mother's way while she continues giving birth. Keep a supply of evaporated milk on hand for emergency feedings or later weaning. A formula of evaporated milk, corn syrup, and a little water with egg yolk should be warmed and fed in a doll's or baby's bottle if necessary. Or purchase a pet nurser kit to have on hand; these are available in local pet shops. A supplementary feeding often helps weak pups (those that may have difficulty nursing) over the hump. Keep track of birth weights and weekly readings thereafter; this will furnish an accurate record of the pups' growth and health, and the information will be valuable for your veterinarian.

RAISING THE PUPPIES

After the puppies have been born, take the mother outside for a walk and drink of water, and then leave her to take care of her brood. She will probably not want to stay away more than a minute or two for the first few weeks. Be sure to keep water available at all times and feed her milk or broth frequently, as she needs liquids to produce milk. Encourage her to eat, with her favorite foods, until she seeks it of her own accord. She will soon develop a ravenous appetite and should have at least two large meals a day, with dry food available in addition. Your veterinarian can guide you on the finer points of nutrition as they apply to nursing dams.

Prepare a warm place to put the puppies after they are born

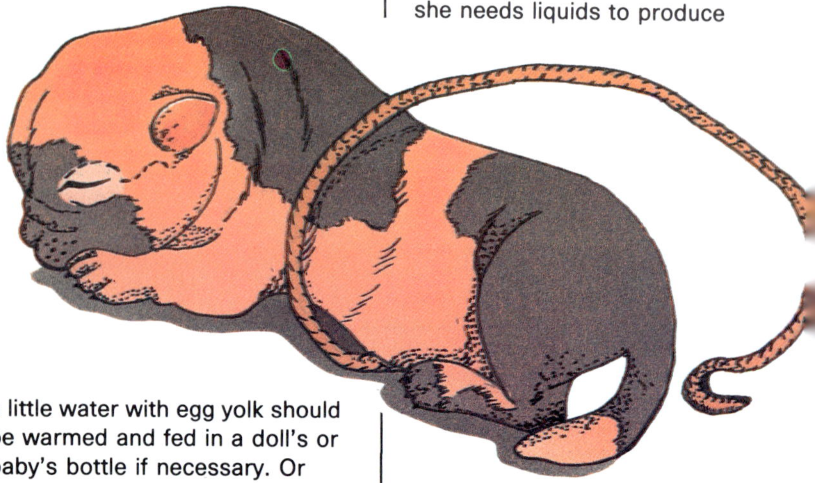

Usually the mother will use her teeth to cut the puppy's umbilical cord. If she fails to do this, you must intervene with sterilized forceps.

to keep them dry and help them to a good start in life. An electric heating pad or hot water bottle covered with flannel can be placed in the bottom of a cardboard box and near the mother so that she can see her puppies. She will usually allow you to help her care for the youngsters, but don't take them out of her sight. Let her handle things if your interference seems to make her nervous.

Be sure that all the puppies are getting enough to eat. If the mother sits or stands instead of lying still to nurse, the probable cause is scratching from the puppies' nails. You can remedy this by clipping them, as you would the bitch's, with a pet nail clipper. Or manicure scissors will do for these tiny claws. Some breeders advise disposing of the smaller or weaker pups in a large litter, as the mother has trouble handling more than six or seven. You can help her out by preparing an extra puppy box or basket furnished with a heating pad and some bedding material. Leave half the litter with the mother and the other half in the extra box, changing off at two-hour intervals at first. Later you may exchange them less frequently, leaving them all together except during the day. Try supplementary feedings, too; as soon as their eyes open, at about two weeks, they will lap from a small dish.

WEANING THE PUPPIES

Normally the puppies should be completely weaned at five weeks, although you can start to feed them at three weeks. They will find it easier to lap semi-solid food than to drink milk at first, so mix baby cereal with whole or evaporated milk, warmed to body temperature, and offer it to the puppies in a saucer. Until they learn to lap it, it is best to feed one or two at a time because they are more likely to walk into it than to eat it. Hold the saucer at their chin level, and let them gather around, keeping paws out of the dish. A damp sponge afterward prevents most of the

Pet nurser kits are sold in pet shops everywhere. If you have to hand feed puppies, check with a veterinarian on how best to do this.

cereal from sticking to the skin if the mother doesn't clean them up. Once they have gotten the idea, broth or babies' meat soup may be alternated with milk, and you can start them on finely chopped meat. At about four weeks, they will eat four meals a day and soon do without their mother entirely. Start them on canned dog food, or leave dry puppy food with them in a dish for self-feeding. Don't leave water with them all the time; at this age everything is a play toy and they will use it as a wading pool. They can drink all they need if it is offered several times a day, after meals. As the puppies grow up the mother will go into their "pen" only to nurse them, first sitting up and then standing. To dry up her milk supply completely, keep the mother away for longer periods; after a few days of part-time nursing she can stay away for even longer periods, and then permanently. The little milk left will be resorbed by her body.

The puppies may be put outside during the day, unless it is too cold or rainy, as soon as their eyes are open. They will benefit from the sunlight. A rubber mat or newspapers underneath will protect them from cold or dampness. As they mature, the pups can be let out for longer intervals, although make sure you provide them with a shelter at night or in bad weather. By now, cleaning up after the matured youngsters is a man-sized job, so put them out at least during the day and make your task easier. If you enclose them in a run or kennel, remember to clean it *daily,* as various parasites and other infectious organisms may be lurking if the quarters are kept dirty.

You can expect the pups to need at least one worming before they are ready to go to new homes; so for each animal, before they are three weeks old, take a stool sample to your veterinarian. The vet can determine, by analyzing the stool, if any of the pups have worms—and if so, what kind of worms are present. If one puppy is infected then all should be wormed as a preventive measure. Follow the veterinarian's advice; this also applies to vaccinations. If you plan to keep a pup yourself, you will want to vaccinate him, and his littermates, at the earliest age. This way, those pups destined for new homes will be protected against some of the more debilitating canine diseases.

THE DECISION TO SPAY OR NEUTER

If you decide not to use your male or female for breeding, or if you are obligated to have the animal altered based on an agreement made between you and the seller, make the necessary arrangements with your veterinarian as soon as possible. The surgery involved for both males and females is relatively simple and painless: males will be castrated and females will have their ovaries and uterus removed. In both cases, the operation does not alter their personalities; you will, however, notice that males will be less likely to roam, to get into fights with other male dogs, and to mount objects and people. From a pet owner's point of view, an animal that is less anxious and less inclined to wander off in search of a mate makes a better companion.

Your veterinarian can best determine at what age neutering or spaying should be done. With a young female dog, the operation may be somewhat more involved, and as a result be more costly; however, in the long run you will be glad you made the decision to have this done for your pet. After a night or two at the veterinarian's or an animal hospital, your bitch can be safely returned to your home. Her stitches will heal in a short time, and when they are removed, you will hardly notice her souvenir scar of the routine operation. Once she has been spayed, she no longer will be capable of having a litter of puppies.

Check with your city or town or with the local humane society for special programs that are available for pet owners. In many municipalities you can have your pet altered for just a small fee; the low price is meant to encourage pet owners to take advantage of this important means of birth control for their dogs. Pet adoption agencies and other animal welfare organizations can house only so many animals at one time, given the money, space, and other resources they have available. This is why pet owners are urged to have their pets altered, so that puppies, resulting from accidental breedings, won't end up being put to sleep as so many others have that are lost, stray, unwanted, or abandoned.

Index

REGISTERED NAME ____ INDIVIDUAL REG. NO. ____ REG. LITTER NO. ____ CALL NAME ____

BREED ____ SEX ____ BORN ____ COLOR AND MARKINGS ____

BREEDER ____ ADDRESS ____ CITY ____ STATE ____

LITTER IDENTIFICATION ____ SOLD TO ____ ADDRESS ____

Our Dog's Pedigree

PARENTS	GRANDPARENTS	GREAT GRANDPARENTS	GREAT GREAT GRANDPARENTS
SIRE ____	SIRE ____	SIRE ____	____ / ____
REG. NO. ____		DAM ____	____ / ____
	DAM ____	SIRE ____	____ / ____
		DAM ____	____ / ____
DAM ____	SIRE ____	SIRE ____	____ / ____
REG. NO. ____		DAM ____	____ / ____
	DAM ____	SIRE ____	____ / ____
		DAM ____	____ / ____

All of the names above are in the father's pedigree.

All of the names below are in the mother's pedigree.

This pedigree is certified to be correct to the best of my knowledge and belief.

Signed ____ *Date* ____ 19 ____